The Westminster Kennel Club Winners

THE WESTMINSTER
KENNEL CLUB
WINNERS 1994

TS-224

© **1994 by T.F.H. Publications, Inc.**

Distributed in the UNITED STATES to the Pet Trade by T.F.H. Publications, Inc., One T.F.H. Plaza, Neptune City, NJ 07753; distributed in the UNITED STATES to the Bookstore and Library Trade by National Book Network, Inc. 4720 Boston Way, Lanham MD 20706; in CANADA to the Pet Trade by H & L Pet Supplies Inc., 27 Kingston Crescent, Kitchener, Ontario N2B 2T6; Rolf C. Hagen Ltd., 3225 Sartelon Street, Montreal 382 Quebec; in CANADA to the Book Trade by Macmillan of Canada (A Division of Canada Publishing Corporation), 164 Commander Boulevard, Agincourt, Ontario M1S 3C7; in ENGLAND by T.F.H. Publications, PO Box 15, Waterlooville PO7 6BQ; in AUSTRALIA AND THE SOUTH PACIFIC by T.F.H. (Australia), Pty. Ltd., Box 149, Brookvale 2100 N.S.W., Australia; in NEW ZEALAND by Brooklands Aquarium Ltd. 5 McGiven Drive, New Plymouth, RD1 New Zealand; in Japan by T.F.H. Publications, Japan—Jiro Tsuda, 10-12-3 Ohjidai, Sakura, Chiba 285, Japan; in SOUTH AFRICA by Multipet Pty. Ltd., P.O. Box 35347, Northway, 4065, South Africa. Published by T.F.H. Publications, Inc.
MANUFACTURED IN THE UNITED STATES OF AMERICA
BY T.F.H. PUBLICATIONS, INC.

THE WESTMINSTER KENNEL CLUB WINNERS 1994

THE WESTMINSTER KENNEL CLUB

Andrew De Prisco, Editor

T. F. H. acknowledges the contribution of Isabelle Francais, whose photographs of the Westminster Bests of Breed make this publication possible. Ninety-five percent of the images in this book actually were produced on site during the 1994 Westminster show.

CONTENTS

Acknowledgments

T.F.H. Publications, Inc., is proud to have produced this commemorative yearbook of the 1994 Westminster Kennel Club Dog Show and wishes to graciously acknowledge the cooperation of President Chester Collier and the Westminster Kennel Club; the editorial assistance of Ms. Mary Bloom; the genuine helpfulness of Rita Lynch and her Westminster staff; Dorie Crowe and the kind folks at M-BF Dog Show Organization, Inc.; photographer Isabelle Français and her staff; assistant photographer W. David Ashbey and other contributing photographers John Ashbey and Chuck Tatham; and the cooperative personnel at Madison Square Garden.

Special thanks to Secretary James P. Crowley and the American Kennel Club for providing detailed AKC records on our Best of Breed winners. All show records published in this volume come directly from the American Kennel Club and are current through January 1994.

We also must acknowledge all the busy and patient handlers of our Best of Breed winners who cooperated with the T.F.H. staff: without your cooperation this book could not have been possible.

Thanks also to Best-in-Show Norwich Terrier Willum, his handler Peter Green and co-owner Ruth Cooper for their continued support.

Finally, to Jaime Gardner, Linda Lindner, Alison Sheehan, Tammy Halaburda, and Nona Kilgore Bauer, for their assistance and ushering the WKC handlers.

T.F.H. Publications, Inc., and The Westminster Kennel Club wish to acknowledge a substantial grant from Nylabone® Products which made this commemorative endeavor possible.

Panoramic aerial view of the 1994 Westminster Kennel Club Dog Show. Photography by John Ashbey.

Preface

The Westminster Kennel Club is pleased to join T.F.H. Publications in the release of the 1994 edition of *The Westminster Kennel Club Winners*. It is our hope that this book will be an important memento of the one hundred eighteenth show and will evoke the wonderful moments and memories of the event. As you can see, the photographs have captured the beauty and harmony and strength of the magnificent dogs that bring the excitement to Westminster. Westminster members are proud of the heritage that is indeed Westminster. The very mention of the name is synonymous with the best in pure-bred dogs in the world.

This year's show brought a total of 2500 pure-bred AKC Champions to Madison Square Garden in New York City. They represented every recognized AKC breed. They came from 49 states, Puerto Rico, Mexico, Central and South America as well as Canada. Visitors and members of the press traveled from all over the world to be present. They were not put off by what were, in fact, the worst snow storms in more than twenty years.

The competition was keen as usual. The depth of quality of the dogs was never greater. The breeders and exhibitors are to be congratulated for a job magnificently done.

With T.F.H. Publications, Westminster hopes your approval of this book will be such that it will become an annual celebration of the best in pure-bred dogs at the Westminster Kennel Club Dog Show.

Chester F. Collier
President
The Westminster Kennel Club

Breed judging of the Working Dogs in progress on the first day of the 1994 Westminster Kennel Club Dog Show. Photography by John Ashbey.

Best in Show judging in progress as Mr. Walter F. Goodman observes James Moses gaiting German Shepherd Dog Ch. Altana's Mystique. Photography by John Ashbey.

BEST IN SHOW:
CHAMPION CHIDLEY WILLUM
THE CONQUEROR

Norwich Terrier Champion Chidley Willum The Conqueror winning Best in Show at The Westminster Kennel Club 1994 under judge Mr. Walter F. Goodman, handled by Peter J. Green. Westminster Kennel Club President Chester F. Collier along with Show Chairman Mr. Ronald H. Mennaker and Mr. Goodman presenting the trophies.

Under the expert handling of terrier man Peter J. Green, Norwich Terrier Champion Chidley Willum the Conqueror achieved the highest award possible in the American dog show world: Best in Show at the Westminster Kennel Club. While Terriers have dominated Westminster since its incipience in 1907, Chidley Willum the Conqueror is the first Norwich Terrier ever to claim the honor of Best in Show.

Willum is owned by Ruth L. Cooper and Patricia P. Lussier-Forrest. Out of Ch. Royal Rock Don of Chidley ex Chidley Chestnuthill's Sprite, he was bred by Karen Anderson and was born on April 11, 1989.

At the tender age of seven months, Willum entered his first of over 300 American Kennel Club shows. Within a month's time, Willum won his very first Best of Breed under Dr. Samuel Draper at the Medina Kennel Club, handled by Beth Sweigart, with

The Making of a Conqueror: Willum on the Way to Westminster

Above: Willum wins his first Best in Show under Australian judge Robert Curtis at the Houston Kennel Club in Spring 1992. **Below:** Best in Show for the second year at the Montgomery County Kennel Club Show, handled by Peter Green, under judge Mrs. Sandra Goose Allen.

whom he finished his championship. Dr. Leon Lussier handled Willum for a short time until Peter Green began specialling Willum in May 1991. With Peter Green, Willum won his first Group under judge Anna Katherine Nicholas at the Middleburg Kennel Club in October 1991. Peter also took Willum to his first Best in Show at the Houston Kennel Club under judge Robert Curtis of Australia in March 1992.

Among Willum the Conqueror's many prestigious victories was Best in Show at the 1992 and 1993 Montgomery County Kennel Club dog show, a highly prized win for any terrier.

By the end of 1993, Champion Chidley Willum the Conqueror had accumulated 310 Bests of Breed, 193 Group firsts out of 250 placements, and 65 Bests in Show.

The 1994 Westminster Kennel Club show marked Willum's first competition at "The Garden," his 66th Best in Show, and his very last dog show. For Peter Green, this victory marked his third Best in Show at Westminster, having previously won with Lakeland Terrier Ch. Stingray of Derryabah, owned by Mr. and Mrs. James A. Farrell, Jr., in 1968 and Sealyham Terrier Ch. Dersade Bobby's Girl, owned by Pool Forge Kennels in 1977. Although Peter regrets losing such a "hell of a good show dog," Willum retired in the grandest style to assume his new favorite role as house dog with his long-time friend and supporter Mrs. Joan Reed.

Peter Green spends a moment with co-owner Ruth Cooper after winning Best in Show at Westminster 1994.

Sporting Group

Judge: Mrs. Betty Wrenn Hoggard.

Group One: Cocker Spaniel (Parti-color)

Ch. Kane Venture Heaven Gait, handled by Jim Sargent. Breeder: Mary S. Meriwether. Owner: John Zolezzi and Debbi Bertrand and J. De Wolfe. Ch. Kane Venture Heaven Gait won his first Best in Show at Klamath DF under Ms. J. Dills in May 1993 and won the Variety at the American Spaniel Club in 1993. The 1994 Westminster Show was his first competition at the Garden.

Group Two: Irish Setter
Ch. Saxonys Evening Reflections
Group Three: Golden Retriever
Ch. Brandymist QB Gal
Group Four: German Shorthaired Pointer
Ch. Wyndbourne's Keepsake

Hound Group
Judge: Mrs. James R. Canalizo.

Group One: Norwegian Elkhound

Ch. Vin-Melca's Marketta, handled by Patricia V. Craige. Breeders: Patricia V. Craige and Carol Frances Anderson. Owners: Jeffrey and Nan Bennet and Patricia V. Craige. Ch. Vin-Melca's Marketta won her first Best in Show under D. Bradley at the Richmond DF in March 1993. She has won 13 Bests in Show and has won the Group 80 times.

Group Two: Petit Basset Griffon Vendéen
Ch. Foxmead's La Belle Sauterelle
Group Three: Beagle, Thirteen Inches
Ch. Lanbur Miss Fleetwood
Group Four: Dachshund (Wirehaired)
Ch. Brazos Ski Solo Wonder W

Working Group
Judge: Mrs. Dorothy N. Collier.

Group One: Boxer

Ch. Hi-Tech's Arbitrage, handled by Jo Anne Sheffler. Breeder: Jo Anne Sheffler. Owners: Dr. and Mrs. William Truesdale. Ch. Hi-Tech's Arbitrage won his first Best in Show at Riverhead Kennel Club under J. Weiss in July 1992. Arbitrage has accumulated 17 Bests in Show and has won the Group 70 times. At his first Westminster Show in 1993, he was awarded Best of Opposite Sex.

Group Two: Portuguese Water Dog
Ch. Rough Seas First Buoy
Group Three: Komondor
Ch. Lajosmegyi Dahu Digal
Group Four: Siberian Husky
Ch. Kontoki's E-I-E-I-O

Terrier Group

Judge: Mr. Robert Condon.

Group One: Norwich Terrier

Ch. Chidley Willum The Conqueror, handled by Peter Green. Breeder: Karen Anderson. Owners: Ruth L. Cooper and Patricia P. Lussier-Forrest. Willum has accumulated 193 Group Firsts and 65 Bests in Show.

Group Two: Fox Terrier (Wire)
Ch. Cunningfox Santeric Patriot
Group Three: Bull Terrier (White)
Ch. Banbury Battersea Of Bedrock
Group Four: Sealyham Terrier
Ch. Farday Glenby Royal Courtesan

Toy Group
Judge: Mr. R. William Taylor.

Group One: Pekingese

Ch. Briarcourt's Damien, handled by David Fitzpatrick. Breeders: David Fitzpatrick. Owner: Nancy H. Shapland. Ch. Briarcourt's Damien won his first Best in Show at the Okaloosa Kennel Club in February 1992 under G. Fancy. He has won the Group 181 times and 45 times Best In Show. He also won the Breed and Group at the 1993 Westminster Kennel Club Show.

Group Two: Toy Poodle
Ch. Appli Dream Of North Well Chako
Group Three: Pug
Ch. Glory's Mumbly Peg
Group Four: Affenpinscher
Ch. Osgood Farm's Mighty Mouse

Non-Sporting Group
Judge: Dr. Jacklyn E. Hungerland.

Group One: Standard Poodle

Ch. La Marka Nina Oscura, handled by Allan Chambers. Breeders: Katherine M. Higgins and Nichole Higgins. Owner: Edward Jenner. Ch. La Marka Nina Obscura won her first Best in Show at the Oakland Kennel Club under Ms. S. Thomas in March 1992. She has won 44 Group Firsts and 12 Bests in Show. At the 1993 Westminster Show, she was awarded Best of Opposite Sex.

Group Two: Miniature Poodle
Ch. Surrey Sweet Capsicum
Group Three: Bichon Frise
Ch. Chaminade Larkshire Lafitte
Group Four: Keeshond
Ch. Windrift's Summertime Blues

Herding Group
Judge: Mr. Stanley S. Saltzman.

Group One: German Shepherd Dog

Ch. Altana's Mystique, handled by James A. Moses. Breeder: M. Charleton. Owner: Jane A. Firestone. Mystique won her first Best in Show at the Beaufort Kennel Club under Dr. Carmen Battaglia. She has won the Group 305 times and has accumulated 192 Bests in Show. She also won the Breed and Group at the 1993 Westminster Kennel Club Show.

Group Two: Bearded Collie
Ch. Brigadoon's Extra Special
Group Three: Collie (Smooth)
Ch. Tedjoi D'Artagnan
Group Four: Bouvier des Flandres
Ch. Quiche's Nite Ryder

BEST JUNIOR HANDLER

Melanie Schlenkert handles Black Cocker Spaniel Ch. Silhouette Special Effects to Best in Junior Showmanship at The Westminster Kennel Club Show. The dog is by Ch. Brookwood Rae's Creek ex Ch. San Jo's Locomotion. Born 12/10/91. Breeder: Linda Pitts and Cheryl Forker. Owners: Elizabeth Mulvey and Melanie Schlenkert. Melanie is 19 years old and lives in Peachtree City, GA. Judges were Mrs. Anne H. Bowes and Mrs. Alice Downey (pictured).

SPORTING DOGS

Three types of gundogs are used by the hunter in the field.

Pointers and Setters locate upland game afield for the hunter by either "pointing" the nose toward the scent, or by "setting" which is assuming a rigid stance.

Retrievers bring killed or wounded game back to the hunter.

Spaniels, long or dense-coated breeds, work close to the gun in rough cover, locating, flushing and retrieving game.

There are 26 breeds or varieties in the Sporting Group:

Brittany
Pointer
Pointer (German Shorthaired)
Pointer (German Wirehaired)
Retriever (Chesapeake Bay)
Retriever (Curly-Coated)
Retriever (Flat-Coated)
Retriever (Golden)
Retriever (Labrador)
Setter (English)
Setter (Gordon)
Setter (Irish)
Spaniel (American Water)
Spaniel (Clumber)
Spaniel, (Cocker) Black
Spaniel, (Cocker) A.S.C.O.B.
Spaniel, (Cocker) Parti-Color
Spaniel (English Cocker)
Spaniel (English Springer)
Spaniel (Field)
Spaniel (Irish Water)
Spaniel (Sussex)
Spaniel (Welsh Springer)
Vizsla
Weimaraner
Wirehaired Pointing Griffon

BRITTANY

Ch. Jordean All Kiddin' Aside

Breeders: Andrea S. and Dennis P. Jordan, DVM. *Owners:* Andrea S. and Dennis P. Jordan, DVM and G.K. Nash (Littleton, CO). *Handler:* Dennis Jordan, DVM. By Ch. Jordean Encore ex Ch. Jordean Millette Just Kiddin'. Born 05/16/89, dog. *Judge:* Mrs. Judith A. Goodin.
AKC Record: 255 Bests of Breed, including Westminster Kennel Club 1992 and 1993; 197 Group placements, including Group 4 Westminster Kennel Club 1993; 45 Bests in Show.

A compact, closely knit dog of medium size, a leggy dog having the appearance, as well as the agility, of a great ground coverer. Strong, vigorous, energetic and quick of movement. In temperament, a happy, alert dog, neither aggressive nor shy. Dogs and bitches, 17½ to 20½ inches, 30 to 40 pounds.

POINTER

Ch. Marjetta Reatta of Kintyre

Breeder: Marjetta Reg. *Owners:* Den & Elsa Lawler (Caro, MI). *Handler:* Cindy T. Lane. By Ch. Marjetta Johnny Appleseed ex Ch. Truewithem Sweet N Sassy. Born 03/31/90, bitch. *Judge:* Mrs. Judith A. Goodin. *AKC Record:* 120 Bests of Breed; 54 Group placements; 2 Bests in Show.

The Pointer is bred primarily for sport afield; he should unmistakably look and act the part. The Pointer's even temperament and alert good sense make him a congenial companion both in the field and in the home. He should be dignified and should never show timidity toward man or dog. Dogs, 25 to 28 inches, 55 to 75 pounds; bitches, 23 to 26 inches, 45 to 65 pounds.

POINTER (GERMAN SHORTHAIRED)

GROUP 4

Ch. Wyndbourne's Keepsake

Breeder: Susan Harrison. *Owner:* Susan Harrison (Ft. Lauderdale, FL). *Handler:* Susan Harrison. By Ch. Wyndbourne's Bustin' Loose ex Ch. Wyndbourne's Remembrance. Born 11/06/89, bitch. *Judge:* Ms. Patricia Webster Laurans.
AKC Record: 106 Bests of Breed, including Westminster Kennel Club 1993; 60 Group placements; 1 Best in Show.

The Shorthair is a versatile hunter, an all-purpose gun dog capable of high performance in field and water. The overall picture which is created in the observer's eye is that of an aristocratic, well-balanced, symmetrical animal with conformation indicating power, endurance and agility and a look of intelligence and animation. Dogs, 23 to 25 inches, 55 to 70 pounds; bitches, 21 to 23 inches, 45 to 60 pounds.

POINTER
(GERMAN WIREHAIRED)

Ch. Windhaven's Cheery Jubilee

Breeders: Jeff, Helen, George and Robert Furlong. *Owner:* Richard and Judith Zaleski (Windmere, FL). *Handler:* Greg Myers. By Ch. Windhaven's Stutzer Stumper ex Ch. Windhaven's Wheel Of Fortune. Born 08/29/89, bitch. *Judge:* Mr. Victor S. Boutwell.
AKC Record: 173 Bests of Breed; 69 Group placements.

The German Wirehaired Pointer is a well muscled, medium sized dog of distinctive appearance. Balanced in size and sturdily built, the breed's most distinguishing characteristics are its weather resistant, wire-like coat and its facial furnishings. Of sound, reliable temperament, the German Wirehaired Pointed is at times aloof but not unfriendly toward strangers; a loyal and affectionate companion who is eager to please and enthusiastic to learn. Dogs, 24 to 26 inches; bitches, smaller but not under 22 inches.

RETRIEVER (CHESAPEAKE BAY)

Ch. Eastern Waters Diamond Dust

Breeder: Nat Horn. *Owner:* Sarah Horn (Woodridge, IL). *Handler:* Nat Horn. By Ch. Riverbends Norgawild Rice II ex Ch. Eastern Waters Royal Topaz. Born 01/10/86, dog. *Judge:* Mr. Victor S. Boutwell. *AKC Record:* 268 Bests of Breed, including Westminster Kennel Club 1993; 103 Group placements; 1 Best in Show.

The Chesapeake dog should show a bright and happy disposition and an intelligent expression, with general outlines impressive and denoting a good worker. Courage, willingness to work, alertness, nose, intelligence, love of water, general quality, and, most of all, disposition should be given primary consideration in the selection and breeding of the Chesapeake Bay dog. Dogs, 23 to 26 inches, 65 to 80 pounds; bitches, 21 to 24 inches, 55 to 70 pounds.

RETRIEVER
(CURLY-COATED)

Ch. Ptarmigan Gale At Riverwatch

Breeder: Janean Marti. *Owners:* Gary E. and Mary Meek (Allegan, MI). *Handler:* Mary Meek. By Ch. Summerwind's Charles Dickens CD ex Ch. Ptarmigan Hard Rain Falling. Born 03/21/91, bitch. *Judge:* Mr. Victor S. Boutwell.
AKC Record: 74 Bests of Breed, including Westminster Kennel Club 1993; 11 Group placements.

A strong smart upstanding dog, showing activity, endurance and intelligence. The Curly Retriever is temperamentally easy to train. He is affectionate, enduring, hardy, and will practically live in the water. Moreover, his thick coat enables him to face the most punishing covert. He is a charming and faithful companion and an excellent guard.

RETRIEVER (FLAT-COATED)

Ch. Adelhard's Quintessence

Breeders: Libby Baarstad and Lana Griffin. *Owners:* Philip and Sandra Park, Libby Baarstad and Lana Griffin (Fredericksburg, VA). *Handler:* William C. Pace III. By Ch. Athercroft Beast Intentions ex Adelhard's Catlin Cantu. Born 06/09/89, bitch. *Judge:* Mr. Victor S. Boutwell.
AKC Record: 90 Bests of Breed; 29 Group placements.

The Flat-Coated Retriever is a versatile family companion hunting retriever with a happy and active demeanor, intelligent expression, and clean lines. Character is a primary and outstanding asset of the Flat-Coat. He is a responsive, loving member of the family, a versatile working dog, multi-talented, sensible, bright and trac- table. As a family companion he is alert and highly intelligent; a lighthearted, affectionate and adaptable friend. He retains the qualities as well as his youthfully good-humored outlook on life into old age. Dogs, 23 to 24½ inches; bitches, 22 to 23½ inches.

RETRIEVER (GOLDEN)

GROUP
3

Ch. Brandymist QB Gal

Breeders: James C. Cobble and Pamela S. Cobble. *Owners:* William and Marie Wingard and James C. and Pamela S. Cobble (Spring Lake, NJ). *Handler:* Michael Faulkner. By Ch. Signature's Sound Barrier ex Ch. Laurell's Up To The Top. Born 11/08/90, bitch. *Judge:* Mr. Thomas H. Bradley III. *AKC Record:* 77 Bests of Breed; 49 Group placements, 2 Bests in Show.

A symmetrical, powerful, active dog, sound and well put together, not clumsy nor long in the leg, displaying a kindly expression and possessing a personality that is eager, alert and self-confident. Primarily a hunting dog, he should be shown in hard working condition. In temperament, friendly, reliable, and trustworthy. Quarrelsomeness or hostility towards other dogs or people in normal situations, or an unwarranted show of timidity or nervousness, is not in keeping with Golden Retriever character. Dogs, 23 to 24 inches, 65 to 75 pounds; bitches, 21½ to 22½ inches, 55 to 65 pounds.

RETRIEVER (LABRADOR)

Ch. Lobuff's Bare Necessities

Breeder: Guide Dog Foundation. *Owners:* B. Shavlik, S. Sasser, L. Agresta and E. Biegel (Goldsboro, NC). *Handler:* Beth Sweigart. By Ch. Dickendall's Ruffy ex Second Sight Brandie. Born 12/06/90, dog. *Judge:* Mr. Thomas H. Bradley III.
AKC Record: 127 Bests in Show, including Westminster Kennel Club 1993; 60 Group placements.

The general appearance of the Labrador should be that of a strongly built, medium-sized, short-coupled dog, possessing a sound, athletic conformation that enables it to function as a retrieving gun dog, the substance and soundness to hunt waterfowl or upland game for long hours under difficult conditions, the character and quality to win

in the show ring, and the temperament to be a family companion. Physical features and mental characteristics should denote a dog bred to perform as an efficient retriever of game with a temperament suitable for a variety of pursuits beyond the hunting environment. True Labrador temperament is as much a hallmark of the breed as the otter tail. The ideal disposition is one of a kindly, outgoing, tractable nature, eager to please and non-aggressive toward man or animal. The Labrador has much that appeals to people; his gentle ways, intelligence and adaptability make him an ideal dog. Dogs, 22½ to 24½ inches, 65 to 80 pounds; bitches, 21½ to 23½ inches, 55 to 70 pounds.

SETTER (ENGLISH)

Ch. Set'R Ridge's Dressed In Gold

Breeders: Jeff Johnson and Melissa D. Johnson. *Owner:* A.L. Polley (Ontario, CN). *Handler:* William Alexander. By Ch. Set'R Ridge's Solid Gold CD ex Ch. Set'R Ridge's Locamotion. Born 11/09/90, dog. *Judge:* Dr. Robert D. Helferty.
AKC Record: 3 Bests of Breed.

An elegant, substantial and symmetrical gun dog, suggesting the ideal blend of strength, stamina, grace, and style. In temperament, gentle, affectionate, friendly, without shyness, fear or viciousness. Dogs, about 25 inches; bitches, about 24 inches.

SETTER (GORDON)

Ch. McMurphy Fieldstone Travis

Breeder: Lesley Andrews. *Owners:* Suzanne Lach and Mary Ann Alston (Scottsdale, AZ). *Handler:* Erica Bandes. By Ch. McMurphy Make Mine Scotch ex Ch. McMurphy's Go For It Gately. Born 01/23/89, dog. *Judge:* Mrs. M. Rosalie Anderson.
AKC Record: 1 Best of Breed.

The Gordon Setter is a good-sized, sturdily built, black and tan dog, well muscled, with plenty of bone and substance, but active, upstanding and stylish, appearing capable of doing a full day's work. The Gordon Setter is alert, gay, interested, and aggressive. He is fearless and willing, intelligent and capable. He is loyal and affectionate, and strong-minded enough to stand the rigors of training. Dogs, 24 to 27 inches, 55 to 80 pounds; bitches, 23 to 26 inches, 45 to 70 pounds.

SETTER (IRISH)

GROUP
2

Ch. Saxonys Evening Reflections

Breeder: Mrs. Jean Roche. *Owners:* Randy Kubacz and Mrs. Jean Roche (Jackson, NJ). *Handler:* Randy Kubacz. By Ch. Scarlly's Red Hot ex Ch. Saxonys Midnite Forget Me Not. Born 07/13/88, dog. *Judge:* Dr. Robert D. Helferty.
AKC Record: 56 Bests of Breed; 27 Group placements; 2 Bests in Show.

The Irish Setter is an active, aristocratic bird dog, rich red in color, substantial yet elegant in build. The Irish Setter has a rollicking personality. Shyness, hostility and timidity are uncharacteristic of the breed. An outgoing, stable temperament is the essence of the Irish Setter. Dogs, 27 inches, about 70 pounds; bitches, 25 inches, about 60 pounds.

SPANIEL
(AMERICAN WATER)

Ch. Lesitas Game Creek Gauge

Breeders: Les Anders and Bonita Anders. *Owner:* Pamela Metts-Boyer (Driggs, ID). *Handler:* Pamela Metts-Boyer. By Ch. His And Hers Gunner's Shadow ex Ch. His And Hers Huntress. Born 12/31/91, dog. *Judge:* Mrs. M. Rosalie Anderson.
AKC Record: 10 Bests of Breed.

The American Water Spaniel was developed in the United States as an all-around hunting dog, bred to retrieve from skiff or canoes and work ground with relative ease. Demeanor indicates intelligence, eagerness to please and friendly. Great energy and eagerness for the hunt yet controllable in the field. Dogs, 15 to 18 inches, 30 to 45 pounds; bitches, 15 to 18 inches, 25 to 40 pounds.

SPANIEL (CLUMBER)

Ch. Raycroft Springsteen TD

Breeder: Mrs. Rae Furness. *Owners:* Dr. Gerard Nash and Janice Friis (Mattawan, MI). *Handler:* Barbara L. Gamache. By Ch. Clubow Star and Strikes at Raycroft ex Outline's Pink Champagne At Raycroft. Born 08/07/89, dog. *Judge:* Mrs. M. Rosalie Anderson.
AKC Record: 176 Bests of Breed; 96 Group placements; 1 Best in Show.

The Clumber is a long, low, heavy dog. His stature is dignified, his expression pensive, but at the same time, he shows great enthusiasm for work and play. The Clumber is a loyal and affectionate dog; sometimes reserved with strangers, but never hostile or timid. Dogs, 19 to 20 inches, 70 to 85 pounds; bitches, 17 to 19 inches, 55 to 70 pounds.

SPANIEL (COCKER) BLACK

Ch. Westglen Blak-Gammon

Breeders: Corliss and Robert Westerman. *Owners:* Corliss Westerman and Tracy Lynn Carroll (Fallbrook, CA). *Handler:* Tracy Lynn Carroll. By Ch. Westglen Blak-A-Tak ex Ch. Canyon Convicted Of Forgery. Born 07/15/89, dog. *Judge:* Mr. Carl J. Anderson.
AKC Record: 191 Bests of Breed, including Westminster Kennel Club 1993; 118 Group placements, including Group 2 Westminster Kennel Club 1993; 21 Bests in Show.

The Cocker Spaniel is the smallest member of the Sporting Group. He is a dog capable of considerable speed, combined with great endurance. Above all he must be free and merry, sound, well balanced throughout, and in action show a keen inclination to work; equable in temperament with no suggestion of timidity. Dogs, 15 inches; bitches, 14 inches.

SPANIEL (COCKER)
A.S.C.O.B.

Ch. LGE's Patek Philippe

Breeder: Linda Gruskin. *Owner:* Linda Gruskin (Ft. Lauderdale, FL). *Handler:* Linda Pitts. By Ch. Crazy Q's Comic Relief ex Ch. Comac Di-Mon Tiara. Born 11/29/92, dog. *Judge:* Mr. Carl J. Anderson. *AKC Record:* 7 Bests of Breed; 2 Group placements.

The Cocker Spaniel is the smallest member of the Sporting Group. He is a dog capable of considerable speed, combined with great endurance. Above all he must be free and merry, sound, well balanced throughout, and in action show a keen inclination to work; equable in temperament with no suggestion of timidity. Dogs, 15 inches; bitches, 14 inches.

SPANIEL (COCKER) PARTI-COLOR

GROUP 1

Ch. Kane Venture Heaven Gait

Breeders: Diana Kane and Sandy Bailey. *Owners:* C. Paul, Sandy Bailey and Diana Kane (Sun River, OR). *Handler:* Jim Sargent. By Ch. Derano's Snowman ex Ch. Ris 'N Star's Francine Kane. Born 12/17/90, dog. *Judge:* Mr. Carl J. Anderson.
AKC Record: 78 Bests of Breed; 27 Group placements; 1 Best in Show.

The Cocker Spaniel is the smallest member of the Sporting Group. He is a dog capable of considerable speed, combined with great endurance. Above all he must be free and merry, sound, well balanced throughout, and in action show a keen inclination to work; equable in temperament with no suggestion of timidity. Dogs, 15 inches; bitches, 14 inches.

SPANIEL
(ENGLISH COCKER)

Ch. Canterbury's Band Of Gold

Breeders: Susan Fiore-McChane and Joann Davis. *Owners:* Susan Fiore-McChane and Joann Davis (Jackson, MI). *Handler:* Robin L. Novak. By Ch. Lochranza Touching Wood ex Ch. Canterbury's I Like Dreaming. Born 08/19/90, bitch. *Judge:* Mrs. E. Irving Eldredge.
AKC Record: 28 Bests of Breed; 5 Group placements.

The English Cocker Spaniel is an active, merry sporting dog, standing well up at the withers and compactly built. He is alive with energy; his gait is powerful and frictionless, capable both of covering ground effortlessly and penetrating dense cover to flush and retrieve game. The English Cocker is merry and affectionate, of equable disposition, neither sluggish nor hyperactive, a willing worker and a faithful and engaging companion. Dogs, 16 to 17 inches, 28 to 34 pounds; bitches, 15 to 16 inches, 26 to 32 pounds.

SPANIEL
(ENGLISH SPRINGER)

Ch. Telltale Eclipse

Breeders: Celie Florence and Delores Streng. *Owners:* Agnes Maiorano and Delores Streng (Jackson, MI).
Handler: Robin L. Novack. By Ch. Telltale Scruples ex Ch. Telltale Autumnfire's Artesian. Born 01/22/90,
dog. *Judge:* Mrs. M. Rosalie Anderson.
AKC Record: 81 Bests of Breed; 39 Group placements; 2 Bests in Show.

The English Springer Spaniel is a medium-size sporting dog with a neat, compact body, and a docked tail. At his best he is endowed with style, symmetry, balance, enthusiasm and is every inch a sporting dog of distinct spaniel character, combining beauty and utility. The typical Springer is friendly, eager to please, quick to learn, willing to obey. Dogs, 20 inches, 49 to 55 pounds; bitches, 19 inches.

SPANIEL (FIELD)

Ch. Woodspoint Jeran Martin

Breeder: Joan Faulkner. *Owners:* James and Lucy Gallagher (Upper Saddle River, NJ). *Handler:* Barbara A. Heckerman. By Ch. Glad Tidings Of Westacres ex Ch. Waterborne Of Westacres. Born 05/24/87, dog. *Judge:* Mrs. M. Rosalie Anderson.
AKC Record: 96 Bests of Breed; 9 Group placements.

The Field Spaniel is a combination of beauty and utility. It is a well balanced, substantial hunter-companion of medium size, built for activity and endurance in heavy cover and water. It has a noble carriage; a proud but docile attitude; is sound and free-moving. Unusually docile, sensitive, fun-loving, independent and intelligent, with a great affinity for human companionship. They may be somewhat reserved in initial meetings. Dogs, 18 inches; bitches, 17 inches.

SPANIEL
(IRISH WATER)

Ch. Poole's Ide Watermark

Breeder: Gregory M. Siner. *Owner:* Gergory M. Siner (Upper Montclair, NJ). *Handler:* Gregory M. Siner. By Ch. Oaktree's Irishtocrat ex Ch. Poole's Ide Oprah O'Reilly. Born 05/06/92, bitch. *Judge:* Mrs. M. Rosalie Anderson.
AKC Record: 9 Bests of Breed; 1 Group placement.

The Irish Water Spaniel presents a picture of a smart, upstanding strongly built sporting dog. Great intelligence is combined with rugged endurance and a bold, dashing eagerness of temperament. Very alert and inquisitive, the Irish Water Spaniel is often reserved with strangers. A stable temperament is essential in a hunting dog. Dogs, 22 to 24 inches, 55 to 65 pounds; bitches, 21 to 23 inches, 45 to 58 pounds.

SPANIEL (SUSSEX)

Ch. Sand Creek's Up to Snuff CDX SH

Breeder: T.L. Murff. *Owners:* Pluis Davern and Judy Murff (Gilroy, CA). *Handler:* Pluis Davern. By Winamar Sand Creek Commander ex Nampara Ashley Lexxfield. Born 08/15/88, dog. *Judge:* Mrs. M. Rosalie Anderson.
AKC Record: 146 Bests of Breed; 45 Group placements; 2 Bests in Show.

The Sussex Spaniel presents a long and low, rectangular and rather massive appearance coupled with free movements and nice tail action. Despite the breed's somber and serious expression, it is friendly and has a cheerful and tractable disposition. Dogs and bitches, 13 to 15 inches, 35 to 45 pounds.

SPANIEL
(WELSH SPRINGER)

Ch. Kris' Rumor Is of DL'Car

Breeder: Kristean R. Von Der Heiden. *Owners:* Darlene K. Ferris and A. Candy Carswell (Milford, CT). *Handler:* A. Candy Carswell. By Ch. DL'Car Fracas Tasmanian D ex Ch. Kris' Lady Polly. Born 01/12/90, dog. *Judge:* Mr. Thomas H. Bradley III.
AKC Record: 46 Bests of Breed; 1 Group placement.

The Welsh Springer Spaniel is a dog of distinct variety and ancient origin. He is an attractive dog of handy size, exhibiting substance without coarseness. The Welsh Springer Spaniel is an active dog displaying a loyal and affectionate disposition. Although reserved with strangers, he is not timid, shy nor unfriendly. To this day he remains a devoted family member and hunting companion. Dogs, 18 to 19 inches; bitches, 17 to 18 inches.

VIZSLA

Ch. Szizlin Bzer

Breeders: Carol Phelps and Bruce Phelps. *Owners:* Ron and Patricia Folz (Woodstock, CT). *Handler:* Alessandra Folz. By Ch. Dirigo Gambler's Marker ex Ch. Heelmark's Ain't She Command'n. Born 06/09/89, dog. *Judge:* Mr. Carl J. Anderson.
AKC Record: 78 Bests of Breed; 19 Group placements.

The Vizsla is a medium-sized short-coated hunting dog of distinguished appearance and bearing. Robust but rather lightly built; the coat is an attractive solid golden rust. This is a dog of power and drive in the field yet a tractable and affectionate companion in the home. A natural hunter endowed with a good nose and above-average ability to take training. Lively, gentle-mannered, demonstrably affectionate and sensitive though fearless with a well developed protective instinct. Dogs, 22 to 24 inches; bitches, 21 to 23 inches.

WEIMARANER

Ch. Norman's Greywind Phoebe Snow

Breeder: Norman F. LeBoeuf. *Owner:* Mrs. Jack L. Billhardt (New Canaan, CT). *Handler:* Stan Flowers. By Ch. Greywind's Jack Frost CD ex Ch. Norman's Easybrae Katie. Born 04/05/90, bitch. *Judge:* Mr. Carl J. Anderson.
AKC Record: 183 Bests of Breed, including Westminster Kennel Club 1993; 135 Group placements; 9 Bests in Show.

A medium-sized gray dog with fine aristocratic features. He should present a picture of grace, speed, stamina, alertness and balance. Above all, the dog's conformation must indicate the ability to work with great speed and endurance in the field. The temperament should be friendly, fearless, alert and obedient. Dogs, 25 to 27 inches; bitches, 23 to 25 inches.

WIREHAIRED POINTING GRIFFON

Ch. Fireside's Rollicking Ruckus

Breeder: Elaine Hunsicker. *Owner:* Joseph Gryskiewicz (Nanticoke, PA). *Handler:* Meg Romanowski. By Ch. Echo De Saint Landry ex Ch. Diana Von Herrenhausen. Born 09/05/91, dog. *Judge:* Mr. Carl J. Anderson.
AKC Record: 59 Bests of Breed; 11 Group placements.

Medium sized, with a noble, square-shaped head, strong of limb, bred to cover all terrain encountered by the walking hunter. His easy trainability, devotion to family, and friendly temperament endear him to all. The nickname of "supreme gundog" is well earned. The Griffon has a quick and intelligent mind and is easily trained. He is outgoing, shows a tremendous willingness to please and is trustworthy. He makes an excellent family dog as well as a meticulous hunting companion. Dogs, 22 to 24 inches; bitches, 20 to 22 inches.

HOUND DOGS

Sporting hounds, man's indispensable partner in the pursuit of game, were developed before man came to depend on firearms. Hounds come in many sizes and shapes, bred for work with game in places as varied as the Arctic and Africa. Basically the hounds are known by how they track game: sight or scent. Afghans, Salukis, and others of the Greyhound family locate their game by sight and with their remarkable speed run it to the ground. Others like the Foxhound, Basset or Bloodhound trail by scent, giving voice all the while so the hunter can follow. Dachshunds kill underground and Otterhounds in the water.

There are 25 breeds or varieties in the Hound Group:

      Afghan Hound
      Basenji
      Basset Hound
      Beagle, Thirteen Inch
      Beagle, Fifteen Inch
      Black and Tan Coonhound
      Bloodhound
      Borzoi
      Dachshund (Longhaired)
      Dachshund (Smooth)
      Dachshund (Wirehaired)
      Foxhound (American)
      Foxhound (English)
      Greyhound
      Harrier
      Ibizan Hound
      Irish Wolfhound
      Norwegian Elkhound
      Otterhound
      Petit Basset Griffon Vendeen
      Pharaoh Hound
      Rhodesian Ridgeback
      Saluki
      Scottish Deerhound
      Whippet

AFGHAN HOUND

Ch. Pahlavi Puttin' On The Ritz

Breeders: Wagner and Kageals. *Owner:* Karen Wagner (York, PA). *Handler:* Karen Wagner. By Shirkden Shazam ex Alarickhan Jehada Pahlavi. Born 09/10/83, dog. *Judge:* Mrs. Deborah R. Lawson. *AKC Record:* 169 Bests of Breed, including Westminster Kennel Club 1987 and 1993; 54 Group placements, including Group 2 Westminster Kennel Club 1987; 4 Bests in Show.

The Afghan Hound is an aristocrat, his whole appearance one of dignity and aloofness with no trace of plainness or coarseness. He has a proudly carried head, eyes gazing into the distance as if in memory of ages past. The striking characteristics of the breed stand out clearly, giving the Afghan Hound the appearance of what he is, a king of dogs, that has held true to tradition throughout the ages. In temperament, aloof and dignified, yet gay. Dogs, 27 inches, about 60 pounds; bitches, 25 inches; about 50 pounds.

BASENJI

Ch. Akuaba's Tornado JC

Breeders: Susan Coe and C. A. Young. *Owner:* Susan Coe (Newtown, PA). *Handler:* Susan Coe. By Ch. Changa's Gala Celebration ex Ch. Young-Kwanza Over the Rainbow. Born 11/17/89, dog. *Judge:* Mr. George Stuart Bell.
AKC Record: 210 Bests of Breed; 118 Group placements; 3 Bests in Show.

The Basenji is a small, short haired hunting dog from Africa. Elegant and graceful, the whole demeanor is one of poise and inquiring alertness. The Basenji hunts by both sight and scent. The Basenji should not bark but is not mute. An intelligent, independent, but affectionate and alert breed. Can be aloof with strangers. Dogs, 17 inches, 24 pounds; bitches, 16 inches, 22 pounds.

BASSET HOUND

Ch. Lil' Creek Briarcrest Top Gun

Breeders: Dotty Christiansen and Knox Williams. *Owners:* Daniel and Julie Jones (Hebron, KY). *Handler:* Daniel Jones. By Ch. Hiflite Briarcrest Extra Man ex Ch. Lil' Creek Uff-Da. Born 06/10/89, dog. *Judge:* Ms. Patricia Webster Laurans.
AKC Record: 142 Bests of Breed, including Westminster Kennel Club 1992; 95 Group placements, including Group 1 Westminster Kennel Club 1992; 4 Bests in Show.

The Basset Hound possesses in marked degree those characteristics which equip it admirably to follow a trail over and through difficult terrain. In temperament it is mild, never sharp or timid. It is capable of great endurance in the field and is extreme in its devotion. Dogs and bitches, not more than 14 inches.

BEAGLE,
NOT EXCEEDING 13 INCHES

GROUP
3

Ch. Lanbur Miss Fleetwood

Breeders: Wade S. Burns and Jon Woodring. *Owners:* Jeffrey Slatkin and Eddie Dziuk (Chantilly, VA). *Handler:* David Roberts. By Ch. Lanbur The Company Car ex Ch. Altar's Lanbur Lacy J. Born 04/17/90, bitch. *Judge:* Ms. Patricia Webster Laurans.
AKC Record: 270 Bests of Breed, including Westminster Kennel Club 1992 and 1993; 217 Group placements, including Group 4 Westminster Kennel Club 1992 and Group 2 Westminster Kennel Club 1993; 40 Bests in Show.

A miniature Foxhound, solid and big for his inches, with the wear-and-tear look of the hound that can last in the chase and follow his quarry to the death. Dogs and bitches, not exceeding 13 inches.
The soft brown eyes of the Beagle betray his warm personality but do not instantly reveal his admirable courage and stamina. The latter qualities are especially important while the Beagle is at work in the field, but in the home no gentler, more trustworthy friend could be found.

BEAGLE,
OVER 13 INCHES BUT
NOT EXCEEDING 15 INCHES

Am. and Can. Ch. Fircone Country Cousin

Breeder: James T. Rosshirt, DVM. *Owners:* Bill and Sue Gear (Ontario, CN). *Handler:* William Alexander. By Ch. Lanbur Coupe De Ville ex Ch. Knolland Rose Bouquet II. Born 05/06/92, dog. *Judge:* Ms. Patricia Webster Laurans.
AKC Record: 3 Bests of Breed.

A miniature Foxhound, solid and big for his inches, with the wear-and-tear look of the hound that can last in the chase and follow his quarry to the death. Dogs and bitches, over 13 inches but not exceeding 15 inches.

The soft brown eyes of the Beagle betray his warm personality but do not instantly reveal his admirable courage and stamina. The latter qualities are especially important while the Beagle is at work in the field, but in the home no gentler, more trustworthy friend could be found.

BLACK AND TAN COONHOUND

Ch. WyEast Wit's End

Breeders: James S. and Kathleen M. Corbett and Margo Sensenbrenner. *Owners:* James S. and Kathleen M. Corbett and Margo Sensenbrenner (Aloha, OR). *Handler:* Kathleen M. Corbett. By Ch. Rookwood Night On The Town ex WyEast Wild Wind. Born 06/01/90, bitch. *Judge:* Ms. Patricia Webster Laurans. *AKC Record:* 152 Bests of Breed, including Westminster Kennel Club 1993; 72 Group placements; 4 Bests in Show.

The Black and Tan Coonhound is first and fundamentally a working dog, a trail and tree hound, capable of withstanding the rigors of winter, the heat of summer, and the difficult terrain over which he is called upon to work. Even temperament, outgoing and friendly. As a working scent hound, he must be able to work in close contact with other hounds. Some may be reserved but never shy or vicious. Dogs, 25 to 27 inches; bitches, 23 to 25 inches.

BLOODHOUND

Ch. Honey Tree's PW Wadsworth

Breeder: Anne D. Schettig. *Owner:* Fritz Schmidt (Delaware, OH). *Handler:* Tom Glassford. By Ch. Be-Coz Sir I C Wellington ex Ch. The Honey Tree's Pad-N-Ton Bear. Born 09/10/89, dog. *Judge:* Mrs. Deborah R. Lawson.
AKC Record: 213 Bests of Breed, including Westminster Kennel Club 1993; 96 Group placements; 3 Bests in Show.

The Bloodhound possesses, in a most marked degree, every point and characteristic of those dogs which hunt together by scent (Sagaces). He is very powerful, and stands over more ground than is usual with hounds of other breeds. In temperament he is extremely affectionate, neither quarrelsome with companions nor with other dogs. His nature is somewhat shy, and equally sensitive to kindness or correction by his master. Dogs, 25 to 27 inches, 90 to 110 pounds; bitches, 23 to 25 inches, 80 to 100 pounds.

BORZOI

Ch. Kyrov's Crescendo

Breeder: Amy L. Sorbie. *Owner:* Amy L. Sorbie (Aurora, CO). *Handler:* Holley Eldred. By Ch. P O S H Echovesna's Islaev ex Ch. Kyrov's Rising Star Nastassja CD. Born 12/31/89, dog. *Judge:* Dr. Robert D. Smith.
AKC Record: 48 Bests of Breed; 19 Group placements.

The Borzoi was originally bred for the coursing of wild game on more or less open terrain, relying on sight rather than scent. The Borzoi should always possess unmistakable elegance, with flowing lines, graceful in motion and repose. Dogs, at least 28 inches, 75 to 105 pounds; bitches, at least 26 inches, 15 to 20 pounds less than dogs.

DACHSHUND (LONGHAIRED)

Ch. Boondox Chaps L.

Breeders: Dan Harrison and Melanie Maurey. *Owners:* Dr. Roger and Deborah Brum and Sherry Snyder (Irvine, CA). *Handler:* Corky Vroom. By Ch. Boondox Panama Jack ex Ch. Rose Farms Hannelore Boondox. Born 08/16/88, dog. *Judge:* Mr. Roy Stenmark.
AKC Record: 174 Bests of Breed, including Westminster Kennel Club 1991 and 1992; 73 Group placements, including Group 3 Westminster Kennel Club 1991.

Low to ground, long in body and short of leg with robust muscular development, the Dachshund is well-balanced with bold and confident head carriage and intelligent, alert facial expression. His hunting spirit, good nose, loud tongue and distinctive build make him well-suited for below-ground work and for beating the bush. His keen nose gives him an advantage over most other breeds for trailing. The Dachshund is clever, lively and courageous to the point of rashness, persevering in above– and below-ground work, with all the senses well-developed. Miniatures, 11 pounds and under; standards, 16 to 32 pounds.

DACHSHUND (SMOOTH)

Ch. Laddland A Wing And A Prayer

Breeders: Kaye Ladd, Iris Love and Liz Smith. *Owners:* Kaye Ladd and Elizabeth A. Patterson (Allendale, NJ). *Handler:* Frances "Cookie" Roush. By Ch. Villanol's Gladi's Lad ex Ch. Laddland Pinch Of Cameo. Born 09/06/90, dog. *Judge:* Mr. Roy Stenmark.
AKC Record: 146 Bests of Breed, including Westminster Kennel Club 1992; 56 Group placements; 1 Best in Show.

Low to ground, long in body and short of leg with robust muscular development, the Dachshund is well-balanced with bold and confident head carriage and intelligent, alert facial expression. His hunting spirit, good nose, loud tongue and distinctive build make him well-suited for below-ground work and for beating the bush. His keen nose gives him an advantage over most other breeds for trailing. The Dachshund is clever, lively and courageous to the point of rashness, persevering in above– and below-ground work, with all the senses well-developed. Miniatures, 11 pounds and under; standards, 16 to 32 pounds.

DACHSHUND (WIREHAIRED)

GROUP 4

Ch. Brazos Ski Solo Wonder W.

Breeders: Kellie Williams and Duan and Evelyn Pettyjohn. *Owners:* Kellie Williams and Duan and Evelyn Pettyjohn (Houston, TX). *Handler:* Carlos J. Puig. By Ch. Canebrake Dorchester Danny W ex Ch. Brazos Ski Teckel Tex Tootsie W. Born 11/17/89, bitch. *Judge:* Mr. Roy Stenmark.
AKC Record: 83 Bests of Breed; 43 Group placements; 2 Bests in Show.

Low to ground, long in body and short of leg with robust muscular development, the Dachshund is well-balanced with bold and confident head carriage and intelligent, alert facial expression. His hunting spirit, good nose, loud tongue and distinctive build make him well-suited for below-ground work and for beating the bush. His keen nose gives him an advantage over most other breeds for trailing. The Dachshund is clever, lively and courageous to the point of rashness, persevering in above- and below-ground work, with all the senses well-developed. Miniatures, 11 pounds and under; standards, 16 to 32 pounds.

FOXHOUND (AMERICAN)

Ch. Kelly Mt. Prime Time

Breeder: J.R. Hicks. *Owners:* James M. and Judy G. Rea (Clarkesville, GA). *Handler:* James M. Rea. By Sand Mtn. Train ex Sand Mtn. Kitty. Born 02/03/90, dog. *Judge:* Dr. Robert D. Smith. *AKC Record:* 94 Bests of Breed; 35 Group placements; 1 Best in Show.

The vital characteristics of any Foxhound are: quality, neither coarse nor overrefined; proper structure, resulting in balance; and activity, based on movement—careful observation of the initial stride often provides the clue. These are essentially packhounds that are docile and friendly, though not overly demonstrative to people; not good family pets, they are rapacious hunting hounds born and bred to follow a scent and they thrive on outdoor kennel life. Dogs, 22 to 25 inches; bitches, 21 to 24 inches.

FOXHOUND (ENGLISH)

Ch. Plum Run Marathon

Breeders: Richard Reynolds and Suzy Reingold. *Owners:* Emily Latimer and Suzy Reingold (Spartanburg, SC). *Agent:* Lisa Jane Alston-Myers. By Mr. Stewart's Cheshire Marksman ex Ch. Plum Run Mirage. Born 04/08/87, dog. *Judge:* Dr. Robert D. Smith.
AKC Record: 59 Bests of Breed, including Westminster Kennel Club 1990; 17 Group placements.

In general appearance, a balanced, symmetrical hound, selected for scenting power, cry, drive, stamina, moderate speed, pack sense and courage. Variation among different packs has been selected for functionally and is based on differences in regional ecologies. In temperament, an intelligent, courageous pack hound of cheerful, determined disposition. Dogs and bitches, 24 inches.

GREYHOUND

Ch. Southwesterns Silver Moon

Breeders: Greg Davis, Roger Owens and Anne and Lisa Tater. *Owners:* Marsha and Johnny Wartell, Greg Davis and Roger Owens (Corpus Christi, TX). *Handler:* Marsha Wartell. By Ch. Shalfleet Stormlight ex Ch. Antoherepisode Frostlite. Born 09/12/90, bitch. *Judge:* Mr. George Stuart Bell. *AKC Record:* 5 Bests of Breed.

Strongly built, upstanding, of generous proportions, elegant, muscular, powerful and symmetrical formation; possessing remarkable stamina and endurance; intelligent, gentle, very affectionate and even tempered. Greyhounds make quiet housedogs and are easily socialized; they are not as shy and retiring as one might expect and do not require a large home to dwell contentedly. Dogs, 65 to 70 pounds; bitches, 60 to 65 pounds.

HARRIER

Ch. Seaview Sun Runner

Breeder: Betty M. Burnell. *Owner:* Betty M. Burnell (Scottsdale, AZ). *Agent:* Traci S. Green. By Ch. Cambridgeshire Callboy ex Ch. Seaviews Star Gazer. Born 10/04/91, dog. *Judge:* Mrs. Deborah R. Lawson.
AKC Record: 33 Bests of Breed; 1 Group placement.

Developed in England to hunt hare in packs, Harriers must have all the attributes of a scenting pack hound. They must be active, well balanced, full of strength and quality, in all ways appearing able to work tirelessly, no matter the terrain, for long periods. Outgoing and friendly, as a working pack breed, Harriers must be able to work in close contact with other hounds. Therefore, aggressiveness towards other dogs cannot be tolerated. Dogs and bitches, 19 to 21 inches.

IBIZAN HOUND

Ch. Cesare's Flying First Class SC

Breeder: Ann M. Hunter. *Owners:* Leslie D. Lucas and Glen E. Brand (Livermore, CA). *Handler:* Leslie D. Lucas. By Ch. Atakah's Flying Cub ex Ch. Hemato's Tallia Of Ishtar. Born 09/11/89, dog. *Judge:* Mrs. Deborah R. Lawson.
AKC Record: 121 Bests of Breed; 18 Group placements.

A hunting dog whose quarry is primarily rabbits, this ancient hound was bred for thousands of years with function being of prime importance. Lithe and racy, the Ibizan possesses a deerlike elegance combined with the power of a hunter. The Ibizan is even-tempered, affectionate and loyal. Extremely versatile and trainable, he makes an excellent family pet, and is well suited to the breed ring, obedience, tracking and lure-coursing. He exhibits a keen, natural hunting instinct with much determination and stamina in the field. Dogs, 23½ to 27½ inches, 50 pounds; bitches, 22 ½ to 26 inches, 45 pounds.

IRISH WOLFHOUND

Am. and Can. Ch. Dundrums Sir Chauncy O'Mally

Breeder: Robin A. Kirtley. *Owners:* Richard and Linda Beluscak (Olmsted Falls, OH). *Handler:* Bobbie Barlow. By Superstar In Town ex Ch. Dundrum's Pog Mo Thoin. Born 02/24/89, dog. *Judge:* Mrs. Gayle Bontecou.
AKC Record: 86 Bests of Breed; 13 Group placements.

Of great size and commanding appearance, the Irish Wolfhound is remarkable in combining power and swiftness with keen sight. The largest and tallest of the galloping hounds, in general type he is a rough-coated Greyhoundlike breed. Dogs, minimum of 32 inches and 120 pounds; bitches, minimum of 30 inches and 105 pounds.

The habitat of most Irish Wolfhounds bred in this century has been the private home where his quiet manners, gentle nature and comfortable sense of companionship have made it a natural one.

NORWEGIAN ELKHOUND

Ch. Vin-Melca's Marketta

Breeders: Patricia V. Craige and Carol Frances Andersen. *Owners:* Jeffrey Bennett and Nan Eisley-Bennett and Patricia V. Craige (Carmel, CA). *Handler:* Patricia V. Craige. By Ch. Vin-Melca's Bombardier ex Ch. Vin-Melca's Calista. Born 01/15/91, bitch. *Judge:* Mr. George Stuart Bell.
AKC Record: 126 Bests of Breed; 109 Group placements; 13 Bests in Show.

The Norwegian Elkhound is a hardy gray hunting dog, a square and athletic member of the northern dog family. His unique coloring, weather resistant coat and stable disposition make him an ideal multipurpose dog at work and play. As a hunter, the Norwegian Elkhound has the courage, agility and stamina to hold moose and other big game at bay by barking and dodging attack, and the endurance to track for long hours in all weather over rough and varied terrain. In temperament, the Norwegian Elkhound is bold and energetic, an effective guardian yet normally friendly, with great dignity and independence of character. Dogs, 20½ inches, about 55 pounds; bitches, 19½ inches, about 48 pounds.

OTTERHOUND

Ch. Rinjans Knight De Mon Plaisir

Breeder: JoAnne Coia and Janice Farinon. *Owners:* Jeffrey and Kathleen Baffard (Manchester, CT). *Handler:* Juli Lacey-Ames. By Tar Beach Doubting Thomas ex Ch. Avitar's Old Beauty Of Rinjan. Born 01/08/89, dog. *Judge:* Mrs. Deborah R. Lawson.
AKC Record: 18 Bests of Breed; 2 Group placements.

The Otterhound is a large, rough-coated hound with an imposing head showing great strength and dignity, and the strong body and long striding action fit for a long day's work. It has an extremely sensitive nose, and is inquisitive and perseverant in investigating scents. The Otterhound hunts its quarry on land and water and requires a combination of characteristics unique among hounds. The Otterhound is amiable, boisterous and even-tempered. Dogs, 24 to 27 inches, 75 to 115 pounds; bitches, 23 to 26 inches, 65 to 100 pounds.

PETIT BASSET GRIFFON VENDÉEN

GROUP
2

Ch. Foxmead's La Belle Sauterelle

Breeder: Jane E. Chesmel. *Owner:* Jane E. Chesmel (Keyport, NJ). *Handler:* Mark Threlfall. By Ch. Sirhan Diablotin ex Ch. Sirhan Etoile Filante. Born 12/28/89, bitch. *Judge:* Mrs. Deborah R. Lawson. *AKC Record:* 232 Bests of Breed; 99 Group placements; 1 Best in Show.

The Petit Basset Griffon Vendéen is a scent hound developed to hunt small game over the rough and difficult terrain of the Vendée region. He is bold and vivacious in character; compact, tough and robust in construction. He has an alert outlook, lively bearing and a good voice freely used. In temperament, happy, extroverted, independent, yet willing to please. Dogs and bitches,13 to 15 inches.

PHARAOH HOUND

Ch. K'azar DBL Khanfederate

Breeders: M.C. Durr and Kay Durr. *Owners:* M.C. Durr and Kay Durr (College Station, TX). *Handler:* Shirlee Murray. By Ch. Shema's Ti Khan Deroga ex Ch. Beltara's Twyla Of K'azar. Born 10/08/90, dog. *Judge:* Mrs. Gayle Bontecou.
AKC Record: 114 Bests of Breed; 22 Group placements.

General appearance is one of grace, power and speed. The Pharaoh Hound is medium sized, of noble bearing with hard clean-cut lines—graceful, well balanced, very fast with free easy movement and alert expression. Intelligent, friendly, affectionate, playful and active. Very fast with a marked keenness for hunting, both by sight and scent. Dogs, 23 to 25 inches; bitches, 21 to 24 inches.

RHODESIAN RIDGEBACK

Ch. Ridgelea's Vartan The Master

Breeder: Natalie Bandeian-Zoll. *Owner:* Judith Lichtman (Hamden, CT). *Handler:* Judith Lichtman. By Ch. Wyndrunhr High Veldt Vader ex Ch. Asabi Tyrena Of Ridgelea. Born 03/30/89, dog. *Judge:* Mrs. Gayle Bontecou.
AKC Record: 42 Bests of Breed; 8 Group placements.

The Ridgeback should represent a strong muscular and active dog, symmetrical in outline, and capable of great endurance with a fair amount of speed. The peculiarity of this breed is the ridge on the back, which is formed by the hair growing in the opposite direction to the rest of the coat. A member of the hound family, the Ridgeback is strong-minded and reserved. He can be aggressive with other dogs. He is a splendid companion—obedience training is essential. This is a natural and serious hunter. Dogs, 25 to 27 inches, 75 pounds; bitches, 24 to 26 inches, 65 pounds.

SALUKI

Ch. Ahsanu Noble Shakirah

Breeder: Anne H. Perlow. *Owners:* Melody L. Singleton-Becker and Joseph Becker (Elizabeth, CO).
Handler: Melody Singleton-Becker. By Ch. Bel S'Mbran Promise Of Atallah ex Ch. Calla's Ebony Ice. Born
11/07/91, bitch. *Judge:* Mr. George Stuart Bell.
AKC Record: 31 Bests of Breed; 9 Group placements.

The whole appearance of this breed should give an impression of
grace and symmetry and of great speed and endurance coupled
with strength and activity to enable it to kill gazelle or other quarry
over deep sand or rocky mountains. The expression should be
dignified and gentle with deep, faithful, far-seeing eyes. Dogs, 23
to 28 inches; bitches, considerably smaller.

SCOTTISH DEERHOUND

Ch. Snowden's Roamin' Bridie O' Uplands

Breeder: Jane Hurrell. *Owner:* John D. Hogan (Pawling, NY). *Handler:* John D. Hogan. By Ch. Gayleward's Mo ex Snowden's Silver Nutmeg. Born 11/14/89, bitch. *Judge:* Mrs. Deborah R. Lawson. *AKC Record:* 42 Bests of Breed; 10 Group placements.

A typical Deerhound should resemble a rough-coated Greyhound of larger size and bone. As tall as possible without losing quality. Dogs, 30 to 32 inches and up; bitches, 28 inches and up.
As a companion the Deerhound is ideal, being tractable and easy to train and possessing the most dependable loyalty and utmost devotion to his master.

WHIPPET

Ch. Woodsmoke Wrapped In Rainbows

Breeder: Patricia Miller. *Owner:* Joan G. Damon (Pebble Beach, CA). *Handler:* Mary Dukes. By Woodsmoke's All Ablaze ex Ch. Antares Perlier. Born 03/24/92, bitch. *Judge:* Dr. Robert D. Smith. *AKC Record:* 9 Bests of Breed; 2 Group placements.

A medium size sighthound giving the appearance of elegance and fitness, denoting great speed, power and balance without coarseness. A true sporting hound that covers a maximum of distance with a minimum of lost motion. Amiable, friendly, gentle, but capable of great intensity during sporting pursuits. Dogs, 19 to 22 inches; bitches, 18 to 21 inches.

WORKING DOGS

Although these breeds are sometimes expected to double as hunters, their principal service has been to assist man in his daily work. They have traditionally guarded man's home and his stock, served as drovers, all-around farm dogs and draft animals. Today they also serve as guard dogs, police and border patrol dogs, guide dogs for the blind and dogs of war.

Because of the wide variety of uses for the dogs in this group, there are great differences in appearance. Most, however, are powerfully built and unusually intelligent.

There are 19 breeds in the Working Group:

Akita
Alaskan Malamute
Bernese Mountain Dog
Boxer
Bullmastiff
Doberman Pinscher
Giant Schnauzer
Great Dane
Great Pyrenees
Komondor
Kuvasz
Mastiff
Newfoundland
Portuguese Water Dog
Rottweiler
Saint Bernard
Samoyed
Siberian Husky
Standard Schnauzer

AKITA

Ch. Tobe's Return Of The Jedai

Breeder: Evelyn Geiger. *Owner:* Ruth Winston (Lido Beach, NY). *Handler:* Victor Capone. By Ch. Tobe's Adam Of Genesis ex Ch. Jag's Lois-T. Born 06/21/86, dog. *Judge:* Mrs. Bernard Freeman.
AKC Record: 440 Bests of Breed, including Westminster Kennel Club 1988, 1989, 1990, 1991, 1992, and 1993; 275 Group placements, including Group 2 Westminster Kennel Club 1990 and 1991 and Group 4 Westminster Kennel Club 1992; 21 Bests in Show.

Large, powerful, alert, with much substance and heavy bone. Alert and responsive, dignified and courageous. Aggressive toward other dogs. Dogs, 26 to 28 inches; bitches, 24 to 26 inches.

ALASKAN MALAMUTE

Ch. Nanuke's Colour Me Happy

Breeders: K. Sampson and Sandra D'Andrea. *Owners:* Sandra and Rose Marie D'Andrea (Lockport, NY). *Handler:* Sandra D'Andrea. By Ch. Taolan Flying Colours ex Ch. Nanuke's Karizzma Of Karibou. Born 02/19/91, dog. *Judge:* Mr. Joseph E. Gregory.
AKC Record: 45 Bests of Breed; 21 Group placements; 1 Best in Show.

The Alaskan Malamute is a powerful and substantially built dog with a deep chest and strong, compact body. The Alaskan Malamute is an affectionate, friendly dog, not a "one-man" dog. He is a loyal, devoted companion, playful on invitation, but generally impressive by his dignity after maturity. The Malamute as a sledge dog for heavy freighting is designed for strength and endurance. Dogs, 25 inches, 85 pounds; bitches, 23 inches, 75 pounds.

BERNESE MOUNTAIN DOG

Ch. Abbey Road Here Comes The Sun

Breeder: Deborah J. Wilkins. *Owner:* Deborah J. Wilkins (Prior Lake, MN). *Handler:* Jeff Heim. By Ch. Dallybecks Echo Jackson CD ex Ch. Gruezi Dear Abby CD. Born 02/24/91, dog. *Judge:* Mrs. Bernard Freeman.
AKC Record: 64 Bests of Breed; 5 Group placements.

The Bernese Mountain Dog is a striking, tri-colored, large dog. He is sturdy and balanced. He is intelligent, strong and agile enough to do the draft and droving work for which he was used in the mountainous regions of his origin. The temperament is self-confident, alert and good natured, never sharp or shy. The Bernese Mountain Dog should stand steady, though may remain aloof to attentions of strangers. Dogs, 25 to 27½ inches; bitches, 23 to 26 inches.

BOXER

Ch. Hi-Tech's Arbitrage

Breeder: Jo Anne Sheffler.*Owners:* Dr. and Mrs. William Truesdale (Seekonk, MA). *Handler:* Kimberly A. Pastella. By Ch. Fiero's Tally-Ho Tailo ex Ch. Boxerton Hollyhock. Born 05/08/90, dog. *Judge:* Mr. Joseph E. Gregory.
AKC Record: 202 Bests of Breed; 153 Group placements; 17 Bests in Show.

Developed to serve as guard, working and companion dog, the Boxer combines strength and agility with elegance and style. His expression is alert and temperament steadfast and tractable. Instinctively a "hearing" guard dog, his bearing is alert, dignified and self-assured. With family and friends, his temperament is fundamentally playful, yet patient and stoical with children. Deliberate and wary with strangers, he will exhibit curiosity but, most importantly, fearless courage if threatened. However, he responds promptly to friendly overtures honestly rendered. His intelligence, loyal affection and tractability to discipline make him a highly desirable companion. Dogs, 22½ to 25 inches; bitches, 21 to 23½ inches.

BULLMASTIFF

Ch. Allstar's Nathan Detroit

Breeder: Mimi M. Einstein. *Owners:* Mimi M. Einstein and Jane Hobson (Katonah, NY). *Handler:* Jane Hobson. By Ch. Allstar's Muggsie Malone ex Ch. Allstar's Mae West. Born 01/31/92, dog. *Judge:* Mrs. Jane Roppolo.

In general appearance, that of a symmetrical animal, showing great strength, endurance, and alertness; powerfully built but active. The foundation breeding was 60% Mastiff and 40% Bulldog. The breed was developed in England by gamekeepers for protection against poachers. Fearless and confident yet docile. The dog combines the reliability, intelligence, and willingness to please required in a dependable family companion and protector. Dogs, 25 to 27 inches, 110 to 130 pounds; bitches, 24 to 26 inches, 100 to 120 pounds.

DOBERMAN PINSCHER

Ch. Royalmead's Prescott V Madori

Breeders: Michele B. Bohonak, Ginanna Crouch, DVM and Ann E. Nelson. *Owners:* Ann E. Nelson, Ginanna Crouch, DVM and Joe Reid (Brookshire, TX). *Agent:* Teresa Nail. By Ch. Royalmead's Penny Arcade CD ex Ch. Shadowbriar's Ivy V Royalmead. Born 10/07/89, dog. *Judge:* Mrs. Marilyn Biggs. *AKC Record:* 102 Bests of Breed; 71 Group placements; 6 Bests in Show.

The appearance is that of a dog of medium size, with a body that is square. Compactly built, muscular and powerful, for great endurance and speed. Elegant in appearance, of proud carriage, reflecting great nobility and temperament. Energetic, watchful, determined, alert, fearless, loyal and obedient. Dogs, ideally 27½ inches; bitches, ideally 25½ inches.

GIANT SCHNAUZER

Ch. Stylus' En Vogue

Breeders: Kevin E. Schrum, William P. Shelton and Kyle Steigerwald. *Owners:* Kevin E. Schrum and Kyle Steigerwald (Lake Forest, CA). *Handler:* Kevin E. Schrum. By Ch. Skansen's Notorious Ko v Thief ex Ch. Skansen's Masterpiece. Born 05/15/92, bitch. *Judge:* Mrs. Jane Roppolo.
AKC Record: 11 Bests of Breed; 1 Group placement.

The Giant Schnauzer should resemble, as nearly as possible, in general appearance, a larger and more powerful version of the Standard Schnauzer, on the whole a bold and valiant figure of a dog. Robust, strongly built, nearly square in proportion of body length to height at withers, active, sturdy and well muscled. Temperament combines spirit and alertness with intelligence and reliability. Composed, watchful, courageous, easily trained, deeply loyal to family, playful, amiable in repose, and a commanding figure when aroused. The sound, reliable temperament, rugged build, and dense weather-resistant wiry coat make for one of the most useful, powerful, and enduring working breeds. Dogs, 25½ to 27½ inches; bitches, 23½ to 25½ inches.

GREAT DANE

Ch. Longo's Sweetalk V Michaeldane

Breeders: B. E. Staunton, M. Chiles, C. Gebhardt and Tootie Longo. *Owners:* Joe and Tootie Longo (Mentor On The Lake, OH). *Handler:* Judy A. Harrington. By Ch. Longo's Primo D'Aquino ex Ch. Mikaldane's Put'n On The Ritz. Born 03/29/90, bitch. *Judge:* Mr. Joseph E. Gregory.
AKC Record: 100 Bests of Breed; 44 Group placements; 1 Best in Show.

The Great Dane combines, in its regal appearance, dignity, strength and elegance with great size and a powerful, well-formed, smoothly muscled body. It is one of the giant working breeds, but is unique in that its general conformation must be so well balanced that it never appears clumsy, and shall move with a long reach and powerful drive. It is always a unit—the Apollo of dogs. A Great Dane must be spirited, courageous, never timid or aggressive; always friendly and dependable. Dogs, ideally 32 inches or more; bitches, ideally 30 inches or more.

GREAT PYRENEES

Ch. Pyrless Prime Time

Breeder: Dr. Valerie A. Seeley. *Owners:* Guy and Karen Justin (Monroe, NY). *Handler:* Bob Stebbins. By Ch. Rivergroves Rolling Thunder ex Ch. Pyrless Vera Belle Du Mont. Born 07/25/90, dog. *Judge:* Mrs. Jane Roppolo.
AKC Record: 113 Bests of Breed; 37 Group placements; 1 Best in Show.

The Great Pyrenees dog conveys the distinct impression of elegance and unsurpassed beauty combined with great overall size and majesty. He possesses a keen intelligence and a kindly, while regal, expression. In nature, the Great Pyrenees is confident, gentle, and affectionate. While territorial and protective of his flock or family when necessary, his general demeanor is one of quiet composure, both patient and tolerant. He is strong willed, independent and somewhat reserved, yet attentive, fearless and loyal to his charges both human and animal. Dogs, 27 to 32 inches, 100 pounds and up; bitches, 25 to 29 inches, 85 pounds and up.

KOMONDOR

GROUP
3

Ch. Lajosmegyi Dahu Digal

Breeders: Patricia Turner and Anna Quigley. *Owners:* Patricia Turner and Anna Quigley (Chehalis, WA). *Handler:* Anna Quigley. By Ch. Delwyn Berci ex Ch. Springwater Bit Of Honey. Born 03/15/86, dog. *Judge:* Mrs. Jane Roppolo.
AKC Record: 194 Bests of Breed; 92 Group placements; 3 Bests in Show.

The Komondor is characterized by imposing strength, courageous demeanor, and pleasing conformation. An excellent houseguard. It is wary of strangers. As a guardian of herds, it is, when grown, an earnest, courageous, and very faithful dog. It is devoted to its master and will defend him against attack by any stranger. Because of this trait, it is not used for driving the herds, but only for guarding them. The Komondor's special task is to protect the animals. It lives during the greater part of the year in the open, without protection against strange dogs and beasts of prey. Dogs, 25½ inches; bitches, 23½ inches.

KUVASZ

Ch. Oak Hill's Inanna Of Sumer

Breeders: Nancy McGuire and Janet Kleber. *Owners:* Lynn Brady and C. D. Townsend (Whitmore Lake, MI). *Handler:* William Sahloff. By Lofranco's Amadeus Budavar ex Oakhill's Zaphne Daphne. Born 05/11/91, bitch. *Judge:* Mrs. Estelle B. Cohen.
AKC Record: 134 Bests of Breed; 62 Group placements; 1 Best in Show.

The Kuvasz impresses the eye with strength and activity combined with light-footedness, moving freely on strong legs. A spirited dog of keen intelligence, determination, courage and curiosity. Very sensitive to praise and blame. Primarily a one-family dog. Devoted, gentle and patient with being overly demonstrative. Extremely strong instinct to protect children. Polite to accepted strangers, but rather suspicious and very discriminating in making new friends. Unexcelled guard, possessing ability to act on his own initiative at just the right moment without instruction. Bold, courageous and fearless. Dogs, 28 to 20 inches, 100 to 115 pounds; bitches, 26 to 28 inches, 70 to 90 pounds.

MASTIFF

Ch. Pinehollow Caldedonia's Jackson

Breeders: Nancy Hempel and S. Farber. *Owner:* Nancy Hempel (Clearwater, FL). *Handler:* Thomas Grabe. By Ch. Pinehollow's War Gator ex Caledonia Cameron Pinehollow. Born 08/ 29/91, dog. *Judge:* Mrs. Judith A. Goodin.
AKC Record: 104 Bests of Breed; 28 Group placements; 1 Best in Show.

The Mastiff is a large, massive, symmetrical dog with a well-knit frame. A combination of grandeur and good nature, courage and docility. Dignity, rather than gaiety, is the Mastiff's correct demeanor. Dogs, minimum 30 inches; bitches, minimum 27½ inches.

NEWFOUNDLAND

Ch. Pouch Cove's Darbydale Booker

Breeder: Peggy Helming. *Owners:* Carol Bernard Bergmann and Peggy Helming (Chelsea, MI). *Handler:* Bob Stebbins. By Ch. John's Big Ben of Pouch Cove ex Souvenir of Pouch Cove. Born 03/04/89, dog.
Judge: Mrs. Estelle B. Cohen.
AKC Record: 65 Bests of Breed; 21 Group placements; 1 Best in Show.

The Newfoundland is a sweet-dispositioned dog that acts neither dull nor ill-tempered. He is a devoted companion. A multi-purpose dog, at home on land and in water, the Newfoundland is capable of draft work and possesses natural lifesaving ability. A good specimen of the breed has dignity and proud head carriage. Sweetness of temperament is the hallmark of the Newfoundland; this is the most important single characteristic of the breed. Dogs, 28 inches, 130 to 150 pounds; bitches, 26 inches, 100 to 120 pounds.

PORTUGUESE WATER DOG

GROUP 2

Ch. Rough Seas First Buoy

Breeders: Roughrider Kennels and Cyril and Kathryn Braund. *Owners:* Dr. Lou Guthrie and Steven Bean (Conroe, TX). *Handlers:* Kay Palade and Bobby Schoenfeld. By Ch. Roughrider's Espirito ex Ch. Roughrider's Delta O' Dios Rios CD. Born 11/11/90, dog. *Judge:* Mrs. Judith A. Goodin.
AKC Record: 195 Bests of Breed, including Westminster Kennel Club 1993; 83 Group placements; 2 Bests in Show.

Known for centuries along Portugal's coast, this seafaring breed was prized by fishermen for a spirited, yet obedient nature, and a robust, medium build that allowed for a full day's work in and out of the water. The Portuguese Water Dog is a swimmer and diver of exceptional ability and stamina, who aided his master at sea by retrieving broken nets, herding schools of fish, and carrying messages between boats and to shore. An animal of spirited disposition, self-willed, brave, and very resistant to fatigue. A dog of exceptional intelligence and a loyal companion, it obeys its master with facility and apparent pleasure. Dogs, 20 to 23 inches, 42 to 60 pounds; bitches, 17 to 21 inches, 35 to 50 pounds.

ROTTWEILER

Ch. Roborotts Arco Von Ilco TD

Breeders: Philip and Shelley St. John. *Owners:* Martin and Florence Thomson (Royal Oak, MI). *Handler:* Michael W. Conradt. By Ilco Vom Fusse Der Eifel ex Daggy Vom Bierberger Winkel. Born 05/14/90, dog. *Judge:* Mrs. Marilyn Biggs.
AKC Record: 25 Bests of Breed; 11 Group placements.

The Rottweiler is basically a calm, confident and courageous dog with a self-assured aloofness that does not lend itself to immediate and indiscriminate friendships. A Rottweiler is self-confident and responds quietly and with a wait-and-see attitude to influences in his environment. He has an inherent desire to protect home and family, and is an intelligent dog of extreme hardness and adaptability with a strong willingness to work, making him especially suited as a companion, guardian and general all-purpose dog. Dogs, 24 to 27 inches; bitches, 22 to 25 inches.

SAINT BERNARD

Ch. Lynchcreek's Executive

Breeders: Candace Blancher and Frances S. Porter. *Owners:* Catherine E. Dunphy and Clyde E. Dunphy, DVM (Carlinville, IL). *Handler:* Catherine E. Dunphy. By Ch. Stoan's Knute of Jaz ex Ch. Stoan's Jinny Mae O'Lynchcreek. Born 05/28/91, dog. *Judge:* Mrs. Estelle B. Cohen.
AKC Record: 47 Bests of Breed; 24 Group placements; 1 Best in Show.

Powerful, porportionately tall figure, strong and muscular in every part, with powerful head and most intelligent expression. He is gentle, friendly and easygoing, always acting in a noble manner, Saints can adapt to indoor or outdoor living and need a moderate amount of daily exercise. Dogs, 27½ inches minimum; bitches, 25 inches.

SAMOYED

Ch. Tarahill's Everybody Duck

Breeder: Cheryl A. Wagner. *Owner:* Cheryl A. Wagner (Roswell, GA). *Handler:* Chris Jones. By Ch. Tarahill's Son Of A Duck ex Ch. Tarahill's Can Do Too. Born 09/21/88, dog. *Judge:* Mr. Charles E. Trotter. *AKC Record:* 229 Bests of Breed, including Westminster Kennel Club 1993; 162 Group placements; 11 Bests in Show.

The Samoyed, being essentially a working dog, should present the picture of beauty, alertness and strength, with agility, dignity and grace. Intelligent, gentle, loyal, adaptable, alert, full of action, eager to serve, friendly but conservative, not distrustful or shy, not overly aggressive. Dogs, 21 to 23½ inches; bitches, 19 to 21 inches.

SIBERIAN HUSKY

GROUP
4

Ch. Kontoki's E-I-E-I-O

Breeders: Thomas L. Oelschlager and Marlene A. DePalma. *Owners:* Nan Wisniewski, B. Moye, Thomas L. Oelschlager and Marlene A. DePalma (Brunswick, OH). *Handler:* Thomas L. Oelschlager. By Ch. Rainy Nights Mack-N-Tosh ex Ch. Kontoki's Once Upon A Time. Born 11/05/90, dog. *Judge:* Mrs. Estelle B. Cohen.
AKC Record: 44 Bests of Breed; 33 Group placements; 5 Bests in Show.

The Siberian Husky is a medium-size working dog, quick and light on his feet and free and graceful in action. He performs his function in harness most capably, carrying a light load at a moderate speed over great distances. The characteristic temperament of the Siberian Husky is friendly and gentle, but also alert and outgoing. He does not display the possessive qualities of the guard dog, nor is he overly suspicious of strangers or aggressive with other dogs. Some measure of reserve and dignity may be expected in the mature dog. His intelligence, tractability, and eager disposition make him an agreeable companion and willing worker. Dogs, 21 to 23½ inches, 45 to 60 pounds; bitches, 20 to 22 inches, 35 to 50 pounds.

STANDARD SCHNAUZER

Ch. Cortaillod Ubeda

Breeders: Clive Davies and Mary E. Davies. *Owner:* Carol Boehm (Alberta, CN). *Handler:* Brenda L. Combs. By Ch. Lucky-Devill Van Masatina ex Cortaillod Opportunity Knocks. Born 05/11/89, dog. *Judge:* Mr. Joseph. E. Gregory.
AKC Record: 117 Bests of Breed, including Westminster Kennel Club 1993; 45 Group placements.

The Standard Schnauzer is a robust, heavy-set dog, sturdily built with good muscle and plenty of bone; square-built in proportion of body length to height. The Standard Schnauzer has highly developed senses, intelligence, aptitude for training, fearlessness, endurance and resistance against weather and illness. His nature combines high-spirited temperament with extreme reliability. Dogs, 18½ to 19½ inches; bitches, 17½ to 18½ inches.

TERRIER DOGS

From the Latin word *terra* (earth) comes our word "terrier" describing dogs with stamina, unwavering determination, and courage to go to ground after their game.

The Terriers vary in size and form; bred to route out and kill vermin such as foxes, weasels, and rats, they have been crossed with mastiff breeds to produce hunters and guard dogs with terrier aggressiveness, courage and determination, as well as unmatched loyalty and devotion to their owners.

There are 26 breeds or varieties in the Terrier Group:

Airedale Terrier
American Staffordshire Terrier
Australian Terrier
Bedlington Terrier
Border Terrier
Bull Terrier (Colored)
Bull Terrier (White)
Carin Terrier
Dandie Dinmont Terrier
Fox Terrier (Smooth)
Fox Terrier (Wire)
Irish Terrier
Kerry Blue Terrier
Lakeland Terrier
Manchester Terrier (Standard)
Miniature Bull Terrier
Miniature Schnauzer
Norfolk Terrier
Norwich Terrier
Scottish Terrier
Sealyham Terrier
Skye Terrier
Soft Coated Wheaten Terrier
Staffordshire Bull Terrier
Welsh Terrier
West Highland White Terrier

AIREDALE TERRIER

Ch. Bimindale Bombadil

Breeder: Carol Jaech. *Owner:* Linda Hobbet (Walnut Creek, CA). *Handlers:* Gabriel Rangel and Linda Hobbet. By Ch. Brisline's Blockbuster ex Ch. Bimindale's Augustina. Born 05/21/90, dog. *Judge:* Mrs. Dora Lee Wilson.
AKC Record: 12 Bests of Breed; 1 Group placement.

The Airedale Terrier is an elegant but sturdy dog, well balanced and square with the height at the withers being the same as the length from shoulder point to buttock—appearing neither short in the front legs nor high in the rear. None of the dog's features is exaggerated—the general impression is one of moderation and balance. The expression is eager and intelligent, and the Airedale appears self-confident, unafraid of people or other dogs. Airedales are more reserved in temperament than many of the other breeds, but should not act in a shy manner when approached by strangers. Dogs, approximately 23 inches; bitches, slightly less.

AMERICAN STAFFORDSHIRE TERRIER

Ch. Fraja EC Young Rider

Breeders: John C. McCartney and Kimberly A. Roberts. *Owners:* Yunhee and Kihong Kim (New York, NY). *Handler:* John C. McCartney. By Ch. Fraja EC Ruff Rider ex Ch. Fraja EC Shadow Chaser. Born 10/18/91, dog. *Judge:* Mr. Kenneth M. McDermott.
AKC Record: 6 Bests of Breed; 3 Group placements.

The American Staffordshire Terrier should give the impression of great strength for his size, a well-put-together dog, muscular, but agile and graceful, keenly alive to his surroundings. He should be stocky, not long-legged or racy in outline. His courage is proverbial. Dogs, 18 to 19 inches; bitches, 17 to 18 inches.

AUSTRALIAN TERRIER

Ch. The Farm's Trigger Happy

Breeder: Sheila Dunn. *Owners:* Sheila Dunn and Steve Diuble (Saline, MI). *Handler:* Steve Diuble. By Ch. The Farm's Free Style ex Ch. Yaralla's Tara Sprite. Born 04/04/91, dog. *Judge:* Mrs. Barbara W. Keenan. *AKC Record:* 41 Bests of Breed; 12 Group placements.

A small, sturdy, medium-boned working terrier. As befits their heritage as versatile workers, Australian Terriers are sound and free moving with good reach and drive. Their expression keen and intelligent; their manner spirited and self-assured. The Australian Terrier is spirited, alert, courageous, and self-confident, with the natural aggressiveness of a ratter and hedge hunter; as a companion, friendly and affectionate. Dogs and bitches, 10 to 11 inches.

BEDLINGTON TERRIER

Ch. Liberty's Rain Beau Bleu

Breeder: Desiree Williams. *Owners:* Doug Lehr and Desiree Williams (Pennellville, NY). *Handlers:* Douglas R. Lehr and Dess June. By Ch. Cleo's Baron Of Barrigton ex Ch. Liberty's Georgia On My Mind. Born 08/26/92, dog. *Judge:* Mrs. Barbara W. Keenan.
AKC Record: 14 Bests of Breed; 4 Group placements; 1 Best in Show.

A graceful, lithe, well-balanced dog with no sign of coarseness, weakness or shelliness. In repose the expression is mild and gentle, not shy or nervous. Aroused, the dog is particularly alert and full of immense energy and courage. Noteworthy for endurance, Bedlingtons also gallop at great speed, as their body outline clearly shows. Dogs, 16½ inches; bitches, 15½ inches.

BORDER TERRIER

Ch. Kilduff's Divot Of Braelar

Breeders: Maribeth McMahon and Betsy Finley. *Owner:* Jeanne Lareau (Worcester, MA). *Handlers:* Peter J. Green and Beth Sweigart. By Ch. Woodlawns Rerun O Stonecourt ex Ch. Woodlawn's Clancie O'Kilduff. Born 07/18/89, dog. *Judge:* Dr. M. Josephine Deubler.
AKC Record: 153 Bests of Breed; 20 Group placements.

He is an active terrier of medium bone, strongly put together, suggesting endurance and agility. Since the Border Terrier is a working terrier of a size to go to ground and able, within reason, to follow a horse, his conformation should be such that he be ideally built to do his job. For this work he must be alert, active and agile, and capable of squeezing through narrow apertures and rapidly traversing any kind of terrain. By nature he is good-tempered, affectionate, obedient and easily trained. In the field he is hard as nails, "game as they come" and driving in attack. Dogs, 13 to 15½ pounds; bitches, 11½ to 14 pounds.

BULL TERRIER (COLORED)

Ch. Winsor's In Living Color

Breeders: Marion and Ed Dussault. *Owners:* Karen D. Cooke and Marion Dussault (Woronoco, MA). *Handler:* Karen D. Cooke. By Ch. Windfall's Master Marcus ex Miss Piggy's Peggie. Born 08/23/92, dog. *Judge:* Mr. Kenneth M. McDermott. *AKC Record:* 7 Bests of Breed.

The Bull Terrier must be strongly built, muscular, symmetrical and active, with a keen determined and intelligent expression, full of fire but of sweet disposition and amenable to discipline. Bull Terriers usually exhibit a degree of animation and individuality in the ring. They should not be penalized for their exuberant approach if they are not overly disruptive or aggressive. Bull Terriers live nicely with other animals and are trustworthy with children.

BULL TERRIER (WHITE)

GROUP
3

Ch. Banbury Battersea Of Bedrock

Breeders: Jay and Mary Remer. *Owners:* Jay and Mary Remer and W.E. MacKay-Smith (Villanova, PA). *Handler:* Mary Remer. By Ch. Bullyrock Batteries Included ex Banbury Black Simba Of Bedrock. Born 03/16/91, dog. *Judge:* Mr. Kenneth M. McDermott.
AKC Record: 31 Bests of Breed; 12 Group placements.

The Bull Terrier must be strongly built, muscular, symmetrical and active, with a keen determined and intelligent expression, full of fire but of sweet disposition and amenable to discipline. Bull Terriers usually exhibit a degree of animation and individuality in the ring. They should not be penalized for their exuberant approach if they are not overly disruptive or aggressive. Bull Terriers live nicely with other animals and are trustworthy with children.

CAIRN TERRIER

Am. and Can. Ch. Foxairn Tinman

Breeders: Sanderson and Margaret McIlwain. *Owner:* Betty Hyslop (Ontario, Canada). *Handler:* Peggy Beisel. By Ch. Sharolaine's Kalypso ex Ch. Foxairn Little Miss Marker. Born 12/23/88, dog. *Judge:* Dr. M. Josephine Deubler.
AKC Record: 231 Bests of Breed, including Westminster Kennel Club 1993; 157 Group placements; 3 Bests in Show.

An active, game, hardy, small working terrier of short-legged class. Dogs, 10 inches, 14 pounds; bitches, 9½ inches, 13 pounds. No two Cairns are truly alike: each has distinct personality. As a rule, though, Cairns are somewhat independent. Their intelligence makes them curious and extremely quick to learn. They are surprisingly sensitive, and harsh punishment is not necessary or desirable. Cairns seem to have an inborn affinity for children. Cairns are not suited to living outside. They are far more rewarding pets when they live in close contact with their family.

DANDIE DINMONT TERRIER

Ch. Mar Sher's Schaefer

Breeders: Sharon and Marvin Gelb. *Owners:* Sharon and Marvin Gelb (Monroe, CT). *Handler:* Marvin Gelb. By Ch. Mar-Sher's Dan De Lion ex Ch. Munchkintown's Go Ask Alice. Born 07/05/91, dog. *Judge:* Mrs. Barbara W. Keenan.
AKC Record: 66 Bests of Breed; 9 Group placements.

Originally bred to go to ground, the Dandie Dinmont Terrier is a long, low-stationed working terrier with a curved outline. Independent, determined, reserved and intelligent. The Dandie Dinmont Terrier combines an affectionate and dignified nature with, in a working situation, tenacity and boldness. Dogs and bitches, 8 to 11 inches, 18 to 24 pounds.

FOX TERRIER (SMOOTH)

Ch. Nouveau's Chocolate Mousse

Breeders: Michael and Suzanne Sosne and Ann Keil. *Owners:* Michael and Suzanne Sosne (Caro, MI). *Handler:* Suzanne Sosne. By Ch. Proud Fox Simply Norman ex Ch. Nouveau's Fruti Pebbles. Born 07/21/92, dog. *Judge:* Mr. Kenneth M. McDermott.
AKC Record: 7 Bests of Breed; 2 Group placements.

The dog must present a generally gay, lively and active appearance. He should stand like a cleverly made hunter, covering a lot of ground, yet with a short back. Dogs, not exceeding 15½ inches; bitches, proportionally less.

FOX TERRIER (WIRE)

GROUP 2

Ch. Cunningfox Santeric Patriot

Breeder: Charles J. Cunningham. *Owner:* Kathleen Reges (Los Angeles, CA). *Handler:* Gabriel Rangel. By Ch. Bedlam's The Entertainer ex Ch. Cunningfox Santeric Coventry. Born 09/12/90, dog. *Judge:* Mr. Kenneth M. McDermott.
AKC Record: 56 Bests of Breed; 33 Group placements; 4 Bests in Show.

The dog must present a generally gay, lively and active appearance. He should stand like a cleverly made hunter, covering a lot of ground, yet with a short back. Dogs, not exceeding 15½ inches; bitches, proportionally less.

IRISH TERRIER

Ch. Rough N Ready Rock N Roll

Breeder: Raymond Ruiz. *Owner:* Jim Cassity (Granada Hills, CA). *Handler:* Daniel A. Sackos. By Ch. Tralee's Storm Warning ex Ch. She's Rough N Ready. Born 04/19/88, dog. *Judge:* Mrs. Barbara W. Keenan. *AKC Record:* 326 Bests of Breed, including Westminster Kennel Club 1990 and 1991; 95 Group placements; 1 Best in Show.

He must be all-of-a-piece, a balanced vital picture of symmetry, proportion and harmony. Furthermore, he must convey character. The temperament of the Irish Terrier reflects his early background: he was family pet, guard dog, and hunter. He is good tempered, spirited and game. It is of the utmost importance that the Irish Terrier show fire and animation. There is a heedless, reckless pluck about the Irish Terrier which is characteristic, and which, coupled with the headlong dash, blind to all consequences, with which he rushes at his adversary, has earned for the breed the proud epithet of "Daredevil." He is of good temper, most affectionate, and absolutely loyal to mankind. He is ever on guard, and stands between his home and all that threatens. Dogs, 18 inches, 27 pounds; bitches, 18 inches, 25 pounds.

KERRY BLUE TERRIER

Ch. Travelling Man V Dalenbroek

Breeder: M. C. Heemels-Engelen. *Owners:* Dr. and Mrs. R. A. Reilly (Lakewood, OH). *Handler:* Peter J. Green. By Ch. Geoffrey V. Daelenbroek ex Tiffany Sarah V Daelenbroek. Born 07/01/90, dog. *Judge:* Mrs. Dora Lee Wilson.
AKC Record: 61 Bests of Breed, including Westminster Kennel CLub 1993; 26 Group placements; 1 Best in Show.

The typical Kerry Blue Terrier should be upstanding, well knit and in good balance, showing a well developed and muscular body with definite terrier style and character throughout. The Kerry Blue makes an ideal house pet. A natural hunter, a born retriever and a fine herd dog—he is used for these purposes in the old country. He is not a yapper, and seldom barks. A Kerry Blue remains playful...a real companion...years longer than most breeds. Dogs, 18 to 19½ inches; bitches, 17½ to 19 inches.

LAKELAND TERRIER

Ch. Aurahil Heartlight V Sujawe

Breeders: Den Lawler and Susan Werner. *Owners:* Don and Edna Lawicki and Den and Elsa Lawler (Scottsdale, AZ). *Handler:* Mark Bettis. By Ch. Sujawes Sweet Liberty ex Ch. Foxrun Stormdancer. Born 09/02/91, bitch. *Judge:* Mr. Kenneth M. McDermott.
AKC Record: 17 Bests of Breed; 12 Group placements.

The Lakeland Terrier was bred to hunt vermin in the rugged shale mountains of the Lake District of northern England. He is a small, workmanlike dog of square, sturdy build. The typical Lakeland Terrier is bold, gay and friendly, with a confident, cock-of-the-walk attitude. Shyness, especially shy-sharpness, in the mature specimen, and aggressiveness are to be strongly discouraged. Dogs, 14½ inches, 17 pounds; bitches, 13½ inches.

MANCHESTER TERRIER (STANDARD)

Ch. Salutaire Sweet Talkin' Man CD

Breeder: Myrtle Klensch and C. Ross. *Owner:* Pat Dresser (Medina, OH). *Handler:* Thomas A. Glassford. By Ch. Salutaire Word to the Wise ex Ch. Salutaire Joker Went Wild. Born 04/23/85, dog. *Judge:* Mr. Kenneth M. McDermott.
AKC Record: 464 Bests of Breed, including Westminster Kennel Club 1991, 1992 and 1993; 249 Group placements; 5 Bests in Show.

The Manchester Terrier is neither aggressive nor shy. He is keenly observant, devoted, but discerning. Not being a sparring breed, the Manchester is generally friendly with other dogs. Dogs and bitches, over 12 but not exceeding 22 pounds.

MINIATURE BULL TERRIER

Ch. Bunkie's Luvabull Howdy Doody

Breeder: Trudy Pizer. *Owner:* Marianna Browne (Casco, MI). *Handler:* Bobby Barlow. By Ch. Hobbit's Fire N Ice ex Luvabull Red Hot Chili Pepper. Born 07/10/91, dog. *Judge:* Mr. Kenneth M. McDermott. *AKC Record:* 64 Bests of Breed; 4 Group placements.

The Miniature Bull Terrier must be strongly built, symmetrical and active, with a keen, determined and intelligent expression. He should be full of fire, having a courageous, even temperament and be amenable to discipline. Dogs and bitches, 10 to 14 inches.

MINIATURE SCHNAUZER

Ch. Carolane's Midnight Magician

Breeder: Carol P. Beiles. *Owner:* Carol P. Beiles (Brookville, NY). *Handler:* Landis Hirstein. By Feldmar Night Storm of Jonar ex Ch. Carolanes Nightwatch. Born 10/19/91, dog. *Judge:* Dr. M. Josephine Deubler. *AKC Record:* 21 Bests of Breed; 8 Group placements.

The Miniature Schnauzer is a robust, active dog of terrier type, resembling his larger cousin, the Standard Schnauzer, in general appearance and of an alert, active disposition. The typical Miniature Schnauzer is alert and spirited, yet obedient to command. He is friendly, intelligent and willing to please. He should never be overaggressive or timid. Dogs and bitches, 12 to 14 inches.

NORFOLK TERRIER

Ch. Glendale Gardenparty O Truly

Breeder: Linda Haring. *Owners:* Linda Haring and Howard and Bridget Holzhauser (Sandusky, OH). *Handler:* Roxanne Stamm. By Ch. Greenfield's The Hustler ex Todwil's Pollyana Of Glendale. Born 01/28/92, bitch. *Judge:* Mrs. Dora Lee Wilson.
AKC Record: 7 Bests of Breed.

The Norfolk Terrier, game and hardy, with expressive dropped ears, is one of the smallest of the working terriers. It is active and compact, free-moving, with good substance and bone. With its natural, weather-resistant coat and short legs, it is a "perfect demon" in the field. This versatile, agreeable breed can go to ground, bolt a fox and tackle or dispatch other small vermin, working alone or with a pack. In temperament, alert, gregarious, fearless and loyal. Never aggressive. Dogs, 9 to 10 inches; bitches tend to be smaller.

NORWICH TERRIER

GROUP 1

Ch. Chidley Willum The Conqueror

Breeder: Karen Anderson. *Owners:* Ruth L. Cooper and Patricia P. Lussier (Glenview, IL). *Handler:* Peter J. Green. By Ch. Royal Rock Don Of Chidley ex Chidley Chestnuthill's Sprite. Born 04/11/89, dog. *Judge:* Mrs. Dora Lee Wilson.
AKC Record: 310 Bests of Breed; 250 Group placements; 62 Bests in Show.

The Norwich Terrier, spirited and stocky with sensitive prick ears and a slightly foxy expression, is one of the smallest working terriers. This sturdy descendent of ratting companions, eager to dispatch small vermin alone or in a pack, has good bone and substance and an almost weatherproof coat. A hardy hunt terrier. In temperament, gay, fearless, loyal and affectionate. Adaptable and sporting, they make ideal companions. Dogs and bitches, not exceeding 10 inches, approximately 12 pounds.

SCOTTISH TERRIER

Ch. Gaelforce Post Script

Breeder: Camille R. Partridge. *Owner:* Vandra L. Huber (Woodinville, WA). By Ch. Gladmac's Taliesin The Bard ex Glenlee's Sable Fox. Born 01/22/91, bitch. *Judge:* Mrs. Barbara W. Keenan.
AKC Record: 62 Bests of Breed; 49 Group placements; 1 Best in Show.

The face should wear a keen, sharp and active expression. Both head and tail should be carried well up. The dog should look very compact, well muscled and powerful, giving the impression of immense power in a small size. Dogs, 10 inches, 19 to 22 pounds; bitches, 10 inches, 18 to 21 pounds.

SEALYHAM TERRIER

GROUP
4

Ch. Farday Glenby Royal Courtesan

Breeder: Victor Hansen. *Owner:* Fran Brown (Clovis, CA). *Handler:* Daniel A. Sackos. By Ch. Stonebroke Feather In My Hat ex Ch. Silvery-Moon Devils Kiss. Born 07/22/91, bitch. *Judge:* Mrs. Barbara W. Keenan. *AKC Record:* 67 Bests of Breed; 17 Group placements.

The Sealyham should be the embodiment of power and determination, ever keen and alert, of extraordinary substance, yet free from clumsiness. Dogs and bitches, 10½ inches, 23 to 24 pounds. The Sealyham today is chiefly a companion, but when given the opportunity makes a very good working terrier. He is very outgoing, friendly yet a good house watchdog whose big-dog bark discourages intruders. He is easily trained but more often than not will add his own personal touch to the exercise or trick being taught.

SKYE TERRIER

Ch. Gleanntan T'Roc O'Gibraltar

Breeders: Roxana L. Rohrich and Gleanntan Knis Reg. *Owners:* Roxana L. Rohrich and Gleanntan Knis Reg (Medina, OH). *Handler:* Roxanna L. Rohrich. By Ch. Buffalo Broom O Cowden Knowes ex Ch. Gleanntan D'Sky's D'Limit. Born 01/26/90, dog. *Judge:* Dr. M. Josephine Deubler.
AKC Record: 137 Bests of Breed; 39 Group placements.

The Skye Terrier is a dog of style, elegance and dignity: agile and strong with sturdy bone and hard muscle. Long, low and level—he is twice as long as he is high. In temperament, a typical working terrier capable of overtaking game and going to ground, displaying stamina, courage, strength and agility. Fearless, good-tempered, loyal and canny, he is friendly and gay with those he knows and reserved and cautious with strangers. Dogs, 10 inches; bitches, 9½ inches.

SOFT COATED WHEATEN TERRIER

Ch. Andover All Done With Mirrors

Breeders: Cynthia G. Vogels and Jacqueline Gottlieb. *Owners:* Cynthia G. Vogels and Jacqueline Gottlieb (Littleton, CO). By Ch. Andover Song 'N Dance Man ex Ch. Doubloon's Illusion. Born 07/05/90, dog. *Judge:* Mrs. Dora Lee Wilson.
AKC Record: 61 Bests of Breed; 20 Group placements.

The Soft Coated Wheaten Terrier is a medium-sized, hardy, well balanced sporting terrier, square in outline. He should present the overall appearance of an alert and happy animal, graceful, strong and well coordinated. The Wheaten is a happy, steady dog and shows himself gaily with an air of self-confidence. He is alert and exhibits interest in his surroundings; exhibits less aggressiveness than is sometimes encouraged in other terriers. Dogs, 18 to 19 inches, 35 to 40 pounds; bitches, 17 to 18 inches, 30 to 35 pounds.

STAFFORDSHIRE BULL TERRIER

Ch. Winning Force

Breeder: Mr. A.C. Wood. *Owner:* Michael Goldfarb (Port Washington, NY). *Handler:* John C. McCartney. By Rellim Black Ace ex Jemstone Diamond. Born 01/17/89, dog. *Judge:* Mr. Kenneth M. McDermott. *AKC Record:* 79 Bests of Breed; 8 Group placements.

The Staffordshire Bull Terrier is a smooth-coated dog. It should be of great strength for its size and, although muscular, should be active and agile. From the past history of the Staffordshire Bull Terrier, the modern dog draws its character of indomitable courage, high intelligence, and tenacity. This, coupled with its affection for its friends, and children in particular, its off-duty quietness and trustworthy stability, makes it a foremost all-purpose dog. Dogs, 14 to 16 inches, 28 to 38 pounds; bitches, 14 to 16 inches, 24 to 34 pounds.

WELSH TERRIER

Ch. La Sierra's Lucky Lad

Breeders: R.C. Williams, Jr. and Karen Williams. *Owners:* R.C. Williams, Jr. and Karen Williams (Shingle Springs, CA). *Handler:* Edward Boyes. By Ch. Anasazi Trail Boss ex Ch. Gregmar's Gossip Of La Sierra. Born 04/24/90, dog. *Judge:* Mrs. Dora Lee Wilson.
AKC Record: 102 Bests of Breed; 57 Group placements; 1 Best in Show.

The Welsh Terrier is a sturdy, compact, rugged dog of medium size with a coarse wire-textured coat. The Welsh Terrier is friendly, outgoing to people and other dogs, showing spirit and courage. Intelligence and desire to please are evident in attitude. The Welsh Terrier is a game dog—alert, aware, spirited—but at the same time, is friendly and shows self-control. Dogs, 15 to 15 ½ inches, about 20 pounds; bitches, proportionally smaller.

WEST HIGHLAND WHITE TERRIER

Ch. Aberglen Lucky Lindy

Breeders: Mark and Sally George. *Owners:* Frederick Melville and Mark and Sally George (Sonoma, CA). *Handler:* Sally George. By Ch. Holyrood's Hootman O'Shelly Bay ex Lanarkstone's Winter Solitude. Born 09/23/91. *Judge:* Mrs. Barbara W. Keenan.
AKC Record: 24 Bests of Breed; 16 Group placements.

The West Highland White Terrier is a small, game, well-balanced hardy looking terrier, exhibiting good showmanship, possessed with no small amount of self-esteem. Alert, gay, courageous and self-reliant, but friendly. Dogs, 11 inches; bitches, 10 inches.

TOY DOGS

Bred down to pocket size, Toy dogs are popular in city and suburban households. Their special quality is their diminutiveness which when coupled with healthy bodies and happy temperaments makes them ideally suited as the family pet. They often resemble their larger cousins in miniature form: the Pomeranian, unmistakably a Nordic Dog; the Papillon, a little Spaniel; the Toy Poodle, a tiny replica of dogs once used as retrievers in the field.

There are 20 breeds or varieties in the Toy Group:

Affenpinscher
Brussels Griffon
Chihuahua (Long Coat)
Chihuahua (Smooth Coat)
Chinese Crested
English Toy Spaniel (Blenheim and Prince Charles)
English Toy Spaniel (King Charles and Ruby)
Italian Greyhound
Japanese Chin
Maltese
Manchester Terrier (Toy)
Miniature Pinscher
Papillon
Pekingese
Pomeranian
Poodle (Toy)
Pug
Shih Tzu
Silky Terrier
Yorkshire Terrier

AFFENPINSCHER

GROUP
4

Ch. Osgood Farm's Mighty Mouse

Breeders: Peter A. Fine and Ramona M. Fine. *Owners:* Dr. and Mrs. Brian J. Shack (Nesconset, NY). *Handler:* Peter J. Green. By Ch. Osgood Farm's Bull Market ex Ch. Osgood Farm's Andromeda. Born 11/09/90, dog. *Judge:* Mr. Norman L. Patton.
AKC Record: 236 Bests of Breed; 147 Group placements; 1 Best in Show.

The Affenpinscher is a balanced, little wiry-haired terrier-like toy dog whose intelligence and demeanor make it a good house pet. Originating in Germany, where the name Affenpinscher means "monkey-like terrier," the breed was developed to rid the kitchens, granaries and stables of rodents. In France the breed is described as the *diablotin moustachu* or the moustached little devil. Both these names help to describe the appearance and attitude of this delightful breed. The general demeanor of the Affenpinscher is game, alert and inquisitive with great loyalty and affection toward its master and friends. The breed is generally quiet but can become vehemently excited when threatened or attacked and is fearless toward any aggressor. Dogs and bitches, 9 to 11½ inches.

BRUSSELS GRIFFON

Ch. Cot'N'Wd Cap'N Crunch

Breeder: Priscilla A. Wells. *Owner:* Priscilla A. Wells (Ponca City, OK). *Handler:* Priscilla A. Wells. By Ch. Nichol's You're My Hero ex Ch. Janeff's Sara Lee. Born 11/08/92, dog. *Judge:* Dr. Harry Smith Jr. *AKC Record:* 2 Bests of Breed; 1 Group placement.

A toy dog, intelligent, alert, sturdy, with a thickset, short body, a smart carriage and set-up, attracting attention by an almost human expression. In temperament, the Brussels Griffon is intelligent, alert and sensitive. Full of self-importance. Dogs and bitches, 8 to 10 pounds.

CHIHUAHUA (LONG COAT)

Ch. Simpatica Celeste

Breeder: Patricia A. Holzkopf. *Owner:* Mrs. Keith Thomas (Waukesha, WI). *Handler:* Linda George. By Ch. Ouachitah Beau Chiene ex Ch. Dartan's Gala Resolution. Born 01/27/93, bitch. *Judge:* Mr. Norman L. Patton.
AKC Record: 24 Bests of Breed: 16 Group placements; 1 Best in Show.

A graceful, alert, swift-moving little dog with saucy expression, compact, and with terrier-like qualities of temperament. Dogs and bitches, not to exceed 6 pounds.

American breeders have produced a diminutive dog that has few comparisons, even among other breeds, in size, symmetry, and conformation, as well as intelligence and alertness. Curiously, the Chihuahua is clannish, recognizing and preferring his own kind, and, as a rule, not liking dogs of other breeds.

CHIHUAHUA
(SMOOTH COAT)

Ch. Bolero's Dusky Sky At Whcliff

Breeder: Sheri Woods. *Owners:* Bonnie Thompson and Katherine Giamona (Fairfield, CA). *Handler:* Roberta L. Woodward. By Ch. Dartans Play It Again Sam ex Bolero's Tahiti Sweetie. Born 07/04/91, dog. *Judge:* Mr. Norman L. Patton.
AKC Record: 57 Bests of Breed; 8 Group placements.

A graceful, alert, swift-moving little dog with saucy expression, compact, and with terrier-like qualities of temperament. Dogs and bitches, not to exceed 6 pounds.

American breeders have produced a diminutive dog that has few comparisons, even among other breeds, in size, symmetry, and conformation, as well as intelligence and alertness. Curiously, the Chihuahua is clannish, recognizing and preferring his own kind, and, as a rule, not liking dogs of other breeds.

CHINESE CRESTED

Ch. Gingery's Brandywine

Breeder: Arlene Butterklee. *Owner:* Orville Vaughn (Evans City, PA). *Handler:* Barbara Beissel. By China Crest Adamant Tea Leaf ex Gipez's Mei-Ling. Born 01/18/92, bitch. *Judge:* Mr. Norman L. Patton. *AKC Record:* 65 Bests of Breed; 31 Group placements.

A Toy dog, fine-boned, elegant and graceful. The distinct varieties are born in the same litter. The Hairless with hair only on the head, tail and feet and the Powderpuff, completely covered with hair. The breed serves as a loving companion, playful and entertaining. In temperament, gay and alert. Dogs and bitches, ideally 11 to 13 inches.

ENGLISH TOY SPANIEL
(BLENHEIM & PRINCE CHARLES)

Ch. Cheri-A's Lord Andrew

Breeders: John R. Wood Jr. and Jerome A.M. Elliot. *Owners:* John R. Wood Jr., Mary K. Dullinger-Cunha and Jerome A.M. Elliot (Revere, MA). *Handler:* Mary K. Dullinger-Cunha. By Ch. Oakridges The Chimes ex Ch. Dorkazyl Taffeta. Born 04/01/88, dog. *Judge:* Dr. Harry Smith Jr.
AKC Record: 226 Bests of Breed, including Westminster Kennel Club 1992 and 1993; 118 Group placements; 1 Best in Show.

The English Toy Spaniel is a compact, cobby and essentially square toy dog possessed of a short-nosed, domed head, a merry and affectionate demeanor and a silky, flowing coat. His compact, sturdy body and charming temperament, together with his rounded head, lustrous dark eye, and well cushioned face, proclaim him a dog of distinction and character. The English Toy Spaniel is a bright and interested little dog, affectionate and willing to please. Dogs and bitches, 8 to 14 pounds.

ENGLISH TOY SPANIEL
(KING CHARLES AND RUBY)

Ch. Kis'N Knight Magic

Breeders: John and Sue Kisielewski. *Owner:* Sue Kisielewski (Monroe, VA). *Handler:* Sue Kisielewski. By Ch. Kis'N Karry On Hugo ex Ch. Kis'N Kristina. Born 12/20/91, dog. *Judge:* Dr. Harry Smith Jr. *AKC Record:* 25 Bests of Breed; 4 Group placements.

The English Toy Spaniel is a compact, cobby and essentially square toy dog possessed of a short-nosed, domed head, a merry and affectionate demeanor and a silky, flowing coat. His compact, sturdy body and charming temperament, together with his rounded head, lustrous dark eye, and well cushioned face, proclaim him a dog of distinction and character. The English Toy Spaniel is a bright and interested little dog, affectionate and willing to please. Dogs and bitches, 8 to 14 pounds.

ITALIAN GREYHOUND

Ch. Early Winter At Bo-Bett

Breeder: Carol A. Harris. *Owners:* James R. Gray, MD and Scott R. Thompson (Winder, GA). *Handler:* Davin McAteer. By Ch. Tekoneva's Dario ex Ch. Silver Bluff Indian Summer. Born 05/08/92, dog. *Judge:* Dr. Harry Smith Jr.
AKC Record: 11 Bests of Breed; 5 Group placements.

The Italian Greyhound is very similar to the Greyhound, but much smaller and more slender in all proportions and of ideal elegance and grace. Dogs and bitches, ideally 13 to 15 inches.

JAPANESE CHIN

Ch. Langcroft Black Tie Affair

Breeders: Harold J. Langseth and Marie A. Langseth. *Owners:* Harold J. Langseth and Marie A. Langseth (Everett, WA). *Handler:* Marie Hahnlen Langseth. By Ch. Tosaho Yes Indeed ex Ch. C-Mi Budha Thumb Print-Cess. Born 03/21/89, dog. *Judge:* Dr. Harry Smith Jr.
AKC Record: 103 Bests of Breed; 70 Group placements; 4 Bests in Show.

In general appearance, that of a lively, high-bred little dog with dainty appearance, smart, compact carriage and profuse coat. These dogs should be essentially stylish in movement, lifting the feet high when in action, carrying the tail over the back. In size they vary considerably, but the smaller they are the better, provided type and quality are not sacrificed. Dogs and bitches, either under or over 7 pounds.

MALTESE

Ch. Shanlyn's Rais'N A Raucous

Breeder: Lynda Podgurski. *Owners:* Joseph Joly III, David and Sharon Newcomb and Vicki Abbott (McKinney, TX). *Handler:* Vicki Abbott. By Ch. Shanlyn's Patrick O'Ria ex Borden's Little Ballerina. Born 09/09/91, dog. *Judge:* Mr. William Bergum.
AKC Record: 18 Bests of Breed; 12 Group placements; 2 Bests in Show.

The Maltese is a toy dog covered from head to foot with a mantle of long, silky, white hair. He is gentle-mannered and affectionate, eager and sprightly in action, and, despite his size, possessed of the vigor needed for the satisfactory companion. For all his diminutive size, the Maltese seems to be without fear. His trust and affectionate responsiveness are very appealing. He is among the gentlest mannered of all little dogs, yet he is lively and playful as well as vigorous. Dogs and bitches, under 7 pounds, ideally 4 to 6 pounds.

MANCHESTER TERRIER (TOY)

Ch. Alabiss Jacks Jill

Breeders: Peter J. and Patricia Lapinski. *Owners:* Peter J. and Patricia Lapinski (Port Orange, FL). *Handler:* Greg Myers. By Ch. St. Lazar's Action Jackson ex Alabiss Acapella. Born 10/06/92, bitch. *Judge:* Mr. William Bergum.
AKC Record: 61 Bests of Breed; 17 Group placements.

A small, black, short-coated dog with distinctive rich mahogany markings and a taper style tail. In structure the Manchester presents a sleek, sturdy, yet elegant look, and has a wedge, long and clean head with a keen, bright, alert expression. The Manchester Terrier is neither aggressive nor shy. He is keenly observant, devoted but discerning. Not being a sparring breed, the Manchester is generally friendly with other dogs. Dogs and bitches, not to exceed 12 pounds.

MINIATURE PINSCHER

Ch. Seville In Tempo With Madric

Breeders: Ann Nelsen and Madeline Miller. *Owner:* Ann Nelsen (West Bloomfield, MI). *Handler:* Lynn Salamin. By Ch. Madric's Lasting Impression ex Ch. Madric's Silky Soul. Born 05/23/92, dog. *Judge:* Mr. Melbourne T. L. Downing.
AKC Record: 18 Bests of Breed; 2 Group placements.

The Miniature Pinscher is structurally a well balanced, sturdy, compact, short-coupled, smooth-coated dog. He naturally is well groomed, proud, vigorous and alert. Characteristic traits are his hackney-like action, fearless animation, complete self-possession, and his spirited presence. Dogs and bitches, 10 to 12½ inches.

PAPILLON

Ch. Josandre' Watchmewin

Breeders: Mary Jo Loye and Pearl George. *Owner:* Pat Jones (Roswell, GA). *Handler:* Chris Jones. By Ch. Kavar Touch Of Josandre' ex Ch. Josandre' Mira Mira. Born 02/07/90, dog. *Judge:* Mr. Melbourne T. L. Downing.
AKC Record: 136 Bests of Breed; 43 Group placements.

The Papillon is a small, friendly, elegant Toy dog of fine-boned structure, light, dainty and of lively action; distinguished from other breeds by its beautiful butterfly-like ears. In temperament, happy, alert and friendly. Neither shy nor aggressive. Dogs and bitches, 8 to 11 inches.

PEKINGESE

GROUP
1

Ch. Briarcourt's Damien Gable

Breeder: David Fitzpatrick. *Owner:* Nancy H. Shapland (Champaign, IL). *Handler:* David Fitzpatrick. By Ch. Briarcourt's Coral Gable ex Briarcourt's Cristle Collage. Born 10/20/90, dog. *Judge:* Mr. Norman L. Patton. *AKC Record:* 235 Bests of Breed, including Westminster Kennel Club 1993; 223 Group placements, including Group 1 Westminster Kennel Club 1993; 45 Bests in Show.

The expression must suggest the Chinese origin of the Pekingese in its quaintness and individuality, resemblance to the lion in directions and independence and should imply courage, boldness, self-esteem and combativeness rather than prettiness, daintiness or delicacy. Dogs and bitches, not to exceed 14 pounds.

POMERANIAN

Ch. Finch's He Walks On Water

Breeder: Diane Finch. *Owner:* Diane Finch (Hamilton, NJ). *Handler:* Jackie Rayner. By Finch's Born Sweet Scottie ex Finch's Ambrosa Mystery. Born 08/03/90, dog. *Judge:* Mr. Melbourne T. L. Downing. *AKC Record:* 124 Bests of Breed; 87 Group placements; 4 Bests in Show.

The Pomeranian in build and appearance is a cobby, balanced, short-coupled dog. He exhibits great intelligence in his expression, and is alert in character and deportment. Dogs and bitches, 3 to 7 pounds, ideally 4 to 5 pounds.

POODLE
(TOY)

Ch. Appli Dream Of North Well Chako

Breeder: Hisako Kitai. *Owner:* Norma Strait (Vista, CA). *Handler:* Kaz Hosaka. By Ch. Wissfire Knock On Wood ex Rose Mary Of Beau Fairlady. Born 10/01/91, bitch. *Judge:* Mr. W. Everett Dean Jr. *AKC Record:* 46 Bests of Breed; 25 Group placements; 1 Best in Show.

A very active, intelligent and elegant appearing dog, squarely built, well proportioned, moving soundly and carrying himself proudly. Properly clipped in the traditional fashion and carefully groomed, the Poodle has about him an air of distinction and dignity peculiar to himself. Dogs and bitches, 10 inches and under.

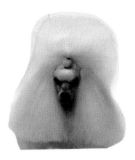

PUG

Ch. Glory's Mumbly Peg

Breeder: Glory Smith. *Owners:* Riney C. and Alicia Kohler (Lodi, CA). *Handler:* Donald E. Rodgers. By Ch. Charlamar's Indian Scout ex Glory's Pop Tart. Born 11/21/90, bitch. *Judge:* Dr. Harry Smith Jr. *AKC Record:* 120 Bests of Breed; 96 Group placements; 3 Bests in Show.

Symmetry and general appearance are decidely square and cobby. This is an even-tempered breed, exhibiting stability, playfulness, great charm, dignity, and an outgoing, loving disposition. Dogs and bitches, 14 to 18 pounds.

SHIH TZU

Ch. Wingate's Tom Terrific

Breeder: Jody Neal. *Owners:* Jody Neal and Yasuyuki Ikeguchi (Huntington Beach, CA). *Handler:* Kristi Trivilino. By Ch. Tu Chu Munchkintown Art Deco ex Wingate's A Star Is Born. Born 04/13/92, dog. *Judge:* Mr. William Bergum.
AKC Record: 18 Bests of Breed; 4 Group placements.

The Shih Tzu is a sturdy, lively, alert Toy dog with long flowing double coat. Befitting his noble Chinese ancestry as a highly valued, prized companion and palace pet, the Shih Tzu is proud of bearing, has a distinctively arrogant carriage with head well up and tail curved over the back. As the sole purpose of the Shih Tzu is that of a companion and house pet, it is essential that its temperament be outgoing, happy, affectionate, friendly and trusting towards all. Dogs and bitches, ideally 9 to 10½ inches; ideally 9 to 16 pounds.

SILKY TERRIER

Ch. Lucknow Local Talent

Breeder: William A. Monteleone. *Owners:* Stephany S. and William A. Monteleone (New Orleans, LA).
Handler: Barbara A. Heckerman. By Ch. Marina's Houston ex Ch. Fawn Hills Lucknow Sweet N' Sour. Born
08/07/89, dog. *Judge:* Dr. Harry Smith Jr.
AKC Record: 196 Bests of Breed, including Westminster Kennel Club 1992; 135 Group placements; 9
Bests in Show.

The Silky Terrier is a true "toy terrier." He is moderately low set,
slightly longer than tall, of refined bone structure, but of sufficient
substance to suggest the ability to hunt and kill domestic rodents.
His inquisitive nature and joy of life make him an ideal companion.
The keenly alert air of the terrier is characteristic. The manner is
quick, friendly, responsive. Dogs and bitches, 9 to 10 inches.

YORKSHIRE TERRIER

Ch. Parkside's The Magic Touch

Breeders: Marie Kaufman-Cardona and Dr. Ivan Cardona. *Owners:* Marie Kaufman-Cardona and Dr. Ivan Cardona (Guaynabo, PR). *Handler:* Sharon Turner. By Ch. Stratford's Magic ex Ch. Marcris My Royal Girl. Born 01/23/90, dog. *Judge:* Mr. William Bergum.
AKC Record: 45 Bests of Breed; 17 Group placements.

In general appearance, that of a long-haired toy terrier whose blue and tan coat is parted on the face and from the base of the skull to the end of the tail and hangs evenly and quite straight down each side of the body. The body is neat, compact and well proportioned. The dog's high head carriage and confident manner should give the appearance of vigor and self-importance. He is very spirited and rather independent—not a lap dog, per se, but a true toy terrier. Dogs and bitches, not to exceed 7 pounds.

NON-SPORTING DOGS

At the earliest dog shows only dogs used for sporting purposes were exhibited. Later, the rarer breeds were shown in what was called a "non-sporting" category. As time went by this group was divided into other categories: the toy dogs, the working dogs, the terriers, and the hounds. The Non-Sporting designation remained for those dogs who outlived their original purpose, such as the Bulldog, developed for bull-baiting, or the Dalmatian, a coach dog. These and other non-sporting dogs are interesting as examples of a heritage from the past.

Though developed for other times, these dogs continue to be among the most popular of breeds.

There are 16 breeds or varieties in the Non-Sporting Group:

Bichon Frise
Boston Terrier
Bulldog
Chinese Shar-Pei
Chow Chow
Dalmatian
Finnish Spitz
French Bulldog
Keeshond
Lhasa Apso
Poodle (Miniature)
Poodle (Standard)
Schipperke
Shiba Inu
Tibetan Spaniel
Tibetan Terrier

BICHON FRISE

Ch. Chaminade Larkshire Lafitte

Breeders: J. O'Dea, Barbara Stubbs and Lois Morrow. *Owner:* Lois Morrow (Westlake Village, CA). *Handler:* Bill McFadden. By Ch. Chaminade LeBlanc Chamour ex Ch. Chaminade Hollyhock Heather. Born 08/10/90, dog. *Judge:* Mr. Nigel Aubrey-Jones.
AKC Record: 224 Bests of Breed, including Westminster Kennel Club 1992 and 1993; 191 Group placements, including Group 1 Westminster Kennel Club 1993; 30 Bests in Show.

The Bichon Frise is a small, sturdy, white powder puff of a dog whose merry temperament is evidenced by his plumed tail carried jauntily over the back and his dark-eyed inquisitive expression. Gentle mannered, sensitive, playful and affectionate in temperament. A cheerful attitude is the hallmark of the breed and one should settle for nothing less. Dogs and bitches, 9½ to 11½ inches.

BOSTON TERRIER

Ch. Debohara RJ's Duff Stuff

Breeder: Joanne L. Hale. *Owners:* Regina Hale and Deborah Thompson (Fayetteville, PA). *Handler:* Norman H. Randall. By Ch. Ancoramn Special Brandywine ex RJ's Peggelo. Born 03/19/90, dog. *Judge:* Mrs. Dawn Vick Hansen.
AKC Record: 60 Bests of Breed; 12 Group placements.

The Boston Terrier is a lively, highly intelligent, smooth coated, short-headed, compactly built, short-tailed, well balanced dog. The dog conveys an impression of determination, strength and activity, with style of a high order; carriage easy and graceful. The Boston Terrier is a friendly and lively dog. The breed has an excellent disposition and a high degree of intelligence, which makes the Boston Terrier an incomparable companion—a most dapper and charming American original. Dogs and bitches, under 15 pounds to not exceeding 25 pounds.

BULLDOG

Ch. Prestwick Gawain

Breeders: Robert and Marla Church. *Owners:* Cody T. Sickle, June Sickle and Robert Church (Merrick, NY). *Handler:* Cody T. Sickle. By Ch. Cherokee Lord Prestwick ex Ch. Jo-Bob's Duchess of Prestwick. Born 08/31/90, dog. *Judge:* Mrs. Sari Brewster Tietjen.
AKC Record: 117 Bests of Breed; 75 Group placements; 5 Bests in Show.

The perfect Bulldog must be of medium size and smooth coat; with heavy, thick-set, low-swung body, massive short faced head, wide shoulders and sturdy limbs. The general appearance and attitude should suggest great stability, vigor and strength. The disposition should be equable and kind, resolute and courageous, and demeanor should be pacific and dignified. These attributes should be countenanced by the expression and behavior. Dogs, about 50 pounds; bitches, about 40 pounds.

CHINESE SHAR-PEI

Ch. Tzo Wens Bijoux

Breeder: Barbara A. LaVere. *Owners:* Barbara and Stephen LaVere (Stanhope, NJ). *Handler:* Mark Therfall. By Ch. Meiting Luv Wun MacMurfee ex Shu-Mai's Right On Target. Born 04/20/92, bitch. *Judge:* Mr. Nigel Aubrey-Jones.
AKC Record: 5 Bests of Breed; 2 Group placements.

An alert, dignified active, compact dog of medium size and substance, square in profile, close-coupled, the well proportioned head slightly but not overly large for the body. The short, harsh coat, the loose skin covering the head and body, the small ears, the "hippopotamus" muzzle shape and the high set tail impart to the Shar-Pei a unique look peculiar to him alone. Regal, alert, intelligent, dignified, lordly, scowling, sober and snobbish, essentially independent and somewhat standoffish with strangers, but extreme in his devotion to his family. The Shar-Pei stands firmly on the ground with a calm, confident stature. Dogs and bitches, 18 to 20 inches, 40 to 55 pounds.

CHOW CHOW

Ch. Sunburst's Rocket Man

Breeders: Harvey Kent and Penny Kent. *Owner:* Hiroshi Matsumo (Lubbock, TX). *Handler:* Michael Brantley. By Ch. Bai-Lee's Promise For Cherie ex Sunburst's French Lace. Born 09/29/92, dog. *Judge:* Mrs. Sari Brewster Tietjen.
AKC Record: 16 Bests of Breed; 6 Group placements.

An ancient breed of northern Chinese origin, this all-purpose dog of China was used for hunting, herding, pulling and protection of the home. While primarily a companion today, his working origin must always be remembered when assessing true Chow type. Keen intelligence, an independent spirit and innate dignity give the Chow an aura of aloofness. It is a Chow's nature to be reserved and discerning with strangers. Displays of aggression or timidity are unacceptable. Dogs and bitches, 17 to 20 inches.

DALMATIAN

Ch. Deltalyn N Penwiper Kis N Cuzn

Breeders: Robert A. and Judith M. Rivard. *Owner:* Mrs. Walter A. Smith (Hamilton, MA). *Handler:* Wendell J. Sammet. By Ch. Alfredrich Handsome Tall 'N Dark ex Deltalyn Lady Legacy. Born 06/12/89, bitch. *Judge:* Mrs. Sari Brewster Tietjen.
AKC Record: 168 Bests of Breed; 144 Group placements; 22 Bests in Show.

The Dalmatian is a distinctively spotted dog; poised and alert; strong, muscular and active; free of shyness; intelligent in expression; symmetrical in outline; and without exaggeration or coarseness. The Dalmatian is capable of great endurance, combined with fair amount of speed. Temperament is stable and outgoing, yet dignified. Dogs and bitches, 19 to 23 inches.

FINNISH SPITZ

Ch. Finkkila's Marsu

Breeders: Tom T. and Marg G. Walker. *Owners:* Tom T. and Marg G. Walker (Bastrop, TX). *Handler:* Clint Livingston. By Ch. Tiko ex Ch. Lokinga's Phoebee. Born 09/26/86, dog. *Judge:* Mrs. Dawn Vick Hansen. *AKC Record:* 90 Bests of Breed; 21 Group placements.

The Finnish Spitz presents a fox-like picture. The breed has long been used to hunt small game and birds. The Finnish Spitz' whole being shows liveliness, which is especially evident in the eyes, ears and tail. Active and friendly, lively and eager, faithful; brave, but cautious. Dogs, 17½ to 20 inches; bitches, 15½ to 19 inches.

FRENCH BULLDOG

Ch. Lefox Goodtime Steel Magnolia

Breeder: Colette V. Secher. *Owner:* Sarah Sweatt (Minneapolis, MN). *Handler:* Jane Flowers. By Ch. Cox's Goodtime Charlie Brown ex Lefox Dolly Parton. Born 12/04/89, bitch. *Judge:* Mrs. Dawn Vick Hansen. *AKC Record:* 272 Bests of Breed, including Westminster Kennel Club 1992 and 1993; 188 Group placements; 6 Bests in Show.

The French Bulldog has the appearance of an active, intelligent, muscular dog of heavy bone, smooth coat, compactly built, and of medium or small structure. Expression alert, curious, and interested. Well behaved, adaptable, and comfortable companions with an affectionate nature and even disposition; generally active, alert and playful, but not unduly boisterous. Dogs and bitches, not to exceed 28 pounds.

KEESHOND

GROUP 4

Ch. Windrift's Summertime Blues

Breeders: Jan Corrington and Joanne Reed. *Owner:* Joanne Reed (Santa Rosa, CA). *Handler:* Joanne Reed. By Ch. Keesland Outlaw ex Ch. Windrift's Stylistic Blues. Born 05/03/91, dog. *Judge:* Mrs. Sari Brewster Tietjen.
AKC Record: 74 Bests of Breed; 40 Group placements; 1 Best in Show.

The Keeshond (pronounced *kayz-hawnd*) is a natural, handsome dog of well-balanced, short-coupled body, attracting attention not only by his coloration, alert carriage, and intelligent expression but also by his stand-off coat, his richly plumed tail well curled over his back, his foxlike expression, and his small pointed ears. In temperament, the Keeshond is neither timid nor aggressive but, instead, is outgoing and friendly with both people and other dogs. The Keeshond is a lively, intelligent, alert and affectionate companion. Dogs, 18 inches; bitches, 17 inches.

LHASA APSO

Ch. Tiblaterr's Ty Breaker

Breeders: Robert and Janie Brewer. *Owners:* Robert and Janie Brewer and Cindy Butsic (Greenville, MI). *Handler:* Cindy Butsic. By Ch. Northwind Mardel Panchan Ty ex Ch. Solitude Mystique O Tara Huff. Born 05/26/89, dog. *Judge:* Mr. Nigel Aubrey-Jones.
AKC Record: 48 Bests of Breed; 13 Group placements.

Gay and assertive, but chary of strangers. Dogs, about 10 to 11 inches; bitches, slightly smaller.

The little Lhasa Apso has never lost his characteristic of keen watchfulness, nor has he lost his hardy nature. These two features should always be developed, since they are of outstanding merit. These dogs are easily trained and responsive to kindness. To anyone they trust they are most obedient, and the beautiful dark eyes are certainly appealing as they wait for some mark of appreciation for their efforts.

POODLE (MINIATURE)

GROUP
2

Ch. Surrey Sweet Capsicum

Breeders: Mrs. J. Furbush, Mrs. J. Clark and Mr. K. Hosaka. *Owner:* Robert A. Koeppel (New York, NY).
Handler: Kaz Hosaka. By Ch. Surrey Jalapeno ex Ch. Surrey In Clover. Born 09/17/91, bitch, *Judge:* Mr.
W. Everett Dean Jr.
AKC Record: 44 Bests of Breed; 37 Group placements; 6 Bests in Show.

A very active, intelligent and elegant appearing dog, squarely built,
well proportioned, moving soundly and carrying himself proudly.
Properly clipped in the traditional fashion and carefully groomed,
the Poodle has about him an air of distinction and dignity peculiar
to himself. Dogs and bitches, over 10 inches to not exceeding 15
inches.

POODLE
(STANDARD)

GROUP
1

Ch. La Marka Nini Oscura

Breeders: Katherine M. Higgins and Nicole Higgins. *Owner:* Edward Jenner (Burlington, WI). *Handler:* Allan Chambers. By Ch. Pamala's Manderley Spellbound ex Ch. Sharbelle Fleur De Lis. Born 03/03/89, bitch. *Judge:* Mr. W. Everett Dean Jr.
AKC Record: 94 Bests of Breed; 67 Group placements; 12 Bests in Show.

A very active, intelligent and elegant appearing dog, squarely built, well proportioned, moving soundly and carrying himself proudly. Properly clipped in the traditional fashion and carefully groomed, the Poodle has about him an air of distinction and dignity peculiar to himself. Dogs and bitches, over 15 inches.

SCHIPPERKE

Ch. Malagold Star Evol Boweebol

Breeders: C. Burek and Michael Starr. *Owners:* Blake and Geri Hart and Michael Starr (DeForest, WI). *Handler:* Geri A. Hart. By Ch. Malagold's Jack's Navoo of J.B. ex Ch. C.J.'s Black Cinder Starr. Born 06/19/91, dog. *Judge:* Mrs. Dawn Vick Hansen.
AKC Record: 28 Bests of Breed; 11 Group placements.

The Schipperke is an agile, active watchdog and hunter of vermin. In appearance he is a small, thickset, cobby, black, tailless dog, with a fox-like face. The Schipperke is curious, interested in everything around him, and is an excellent and faithful little watchdog. He is reserved with strangers and ready to protect his family and property if necessary. He displays a confident and independent personality, reflecting the breed's original purpose as a watchdog and hunter of vermin. Dogs, 11 to 13 inches; bitches, 10 to 12 inches.

SHIBA INU

Ch. Redwing Justa Son Of A Witch

Breeder: Patricia E. Hartman. *Owners:* Patricia E. Hartman and Mary King (Miller Place, NY). *Handler:* Fran Wasserman. By Frerose's Maco Sobi Iwa ex Ch. Frerose Ariel Red Wing. Born 08/01/92, dog. *Judge:* Mrs. Sari Brewster Tietjen.
AKC Record: 11 Bests of Breed.

The Shiba is a small breed dog. He is well balanced, well boned with muscles developed. His moderately compact and well furred body suggests his northern heritage. The Shiba's expression is alert and invites activity. In temperament, inquisitive, good natured, bright, active and slightly aloof at first introduction. Possesses a strong hunting instinct. Dogs, 14½ to 16½ inches, bitches, 13½ to 15½ inches.

TIBETAN SPANIEL

Ch. White Acres Press One

Breeder: White Acres Kennels. *Owners:* Don and Patti Kelley and White Acres Kennels (Maple Valley, WA). *Handler:* Carol Tyte. By Ch. Deetree Lho-Zah-Mi ex Ch. Tibroke's Fiber Optics. Born 07/31/92, dog. *Judge:* Mrs. Dawn Vick Hansen.
AKC Record: 6 Bests of Breed; 3 Group placements.

In general appearance, small, active and alert. The outline should give a well balanced appearance, slightly longer in body than the height at withers. In temperament, gay and assertive, highly intelligent, aloof with strangers. Dogs and bitches, about 10 inches, ideally 9 to 15 pounds.

TIBETAN TERRIER

Ch. Bootiff's Frosty Champagne

Breeders: Joyce Ayotte and S. Lewis-Loomis. *Owner:* Joyce Ayotte (Plattsburgh, NY). *Handler:* Pamela Tillotson-Little. By Ch. Bootiff's Sultim Tenzin ex Ch. Ashante Jasmine. Born 05/29/88, dog. *Judge:* Mrs. Dawn Vick Hansen.
AKC Record: 88 Bests of Breed; 23 Group placements.

The Tibetan Terrier evolved over many centuries, surviving in Tibet's extreme climate and difficult terrain. The breed developed a protective double coat, compact size, unique foot construction, and great agility. The Tibetan Terrier served as a steadfast, devoted companion in all of his owner's endeavors. The Tibetan Terrier is highly intelligent, sensitive, loyal, devoted and affectionate. The breed may be cautious or reserved. Dogs and bitches, 15 to 16 inches, 18 to 30 pounds, average 20 to 24 pounds.

HERDING DOGS

The herding instinct that made the wolf a successful hunter was recognized by man and adapted to his advantage. Domesticated and specialized through selective breeding, they evolved into the herding dogs that made successful farming possible. The great agricultural lands could never have been settled without him, and to this day he works side by side with man. These dogs are agile in movement, anticipating every move, able to turn in an instant, acting on their own or in response to a signal, "eyeing" their flock into obedience. Even those whose versatility extends to working as draft animals or guard dogs may be powerfully built, but never are they cumbersome.

There are 16 breeds or varieties in the Herding Group:

Australian Cattle Dog
Australian Shepherd
Bearded Collie
Belgian Malinois
Belgian Sheepdog
Belgian Tervuren
Bouvier des Flandres
Briard
Collie (Rough)
Collie (Smooth)
German Shepherd Dog
Old English Sheepdog
Puli
Shetland Sheepdog
Welsh Corgi (Cardigan)
Welsh Corgi (Pembroke)

AUSTRALIAN CATTLE DOG

Ch. Imbachs Blue Rebel

Breeder: Marilyn Myers. *Owners:* Linda Bernard and The Ruben Hortas (St. Petersburg, FL). *Handler:* Andrea Glassford. By Ch. Imbachs Paddy Willy ex Ch. C R Aussie Bond. Born 01/16/89, dog. *Judge:* Mrs. Joan Schurr Kefeli.
AKC Record: 147 Bests of Breed; 59 Group placements; 5 Bests in Show.

The general appearance is that of a sturdy, compact, symmetrically-built working dog. With the ability and willingness to carry out any task however arduous, its combination of substance, power, balance and hard muscular condition to be such that must convey the impression of great agility, strength and endurance. The utility purpose is assistance in the control of cattle, in both wide open and confined areas. Ever alert, extremely intelligent, watchful, courageous and trustworhy, with an implicit devotion to duty, making it an ideal dog. Its loyalty and protective instincts make it a self-appointed guardian to the stockman, his herd, his property. Whilst suspicious of strangers, must be amenable to handling in the show ring. Dogs, 18 to 20 inches; bitches, 17 to 19 inches.

AUSTRALIAN SHEPHERD

Ch. Bayshore's Flapjack

Breeder: J. Frank Baylis. *Owner:* J. Frank Baylis (Toms Brook, VA). *Handler:* Amy Grabe. By Ch. Brigadoon's California Dude ex Bayshore's French Toast. Born 10/11/88, dog. *Judge:* Mrs. Joan Schurr Kefeli. *AKC Record:* 100 Bests of Breed; 73 Group placements; 3 Bests in Show.

The Australian Shepherd is a well-balanced dog of medium size and bone. He is attentive and animated, showing strength and stamina combined with unusual agility. The Australian Shepherd is intelligent, primarily a working dog of strong herding and guarding instincts. He is an exceptional companion. He is versatile and easily trained, performing his assigned tasks with great style and enthusiasm. He is reserved with strangers but does not exhibit shyness. Although an aggressive, authoritative worker, the Aussie must not demonstrate viciousness toward people or animals. Dogs, 20 to 23 inches; bitches, 18 to 21 inches.

BEARDED COLLIE

GROUP
2

Ch. Brigadoon's Extra Special

Breeder: Virginia Hanigan. *Owners:* Virginia and Michel Hanigan (Rye, NY). *Handler:* Kathryn Kirk. By Ch. Brigadoon Something Special ex Ch. Brigadoon's Tara Terrific. Born 08/19/89, dog. *Judge:* Mrs. Alice Downey.
AKC Record: 182 Bests of Breed; 116 Group placements; 5 Bests in Show.

The Bearded Collie is hardy and active, with an aura of strength and agility characteristic of a real working dog. Bred for centuries as a companion and servant of man, the Bearded Collie is a devoted and intelligent member of the family. He is stable and self-confident, showing no signs of shyness or aggression. This is a natural and unspoiled breed. Dogs, 21 to 22 inches; bitches, 20 to 21 inches.

BELGIAN MALINOIS

Ch. V Friemann's Spacette

Breeder: John Friemann. *Owner:* Rebecca J. Wasniewski (Cresco, PA). *Handler:* Bob Stebbins. By Ch. Dustivelvet's Astro Spacedog ex Ch. Music's Hawaii O'Crocs-Blancs. Born 02/01/91, bitch. *Judge:* Mrs. Alice Downey.
AKC Record: 71 Bests of Breed; 9 Group placements.

The Belgian Malinois is a well balanced, square dog, elegant in appearance with an exceedingly proud carriage of the head and neck. The breed is confident, exhibiting neither shyness nor aggressiveness in new situations. The dog may be reserved with strangers but is affectionate with his own people. He is naturally protective of his owner's person and property without being overly aggressive. The Belgian Malinois possesses a strong desire to work and is quick and responsive to commands from his owner. Dogs, 24 to 26 inches; bitches, 22 to 24 inches.

BELGIAN SHEEPDOG

Ch. Bel-Reve's Pistolero

Breeders: William G. and Cathy H. Daugherty. *Owners:* William G. and Cathy H. Daugherty (Bethlehem, CT). *Handler:* Gerlinda Hockla. By Ch. Bel-Reve's Carpetbagger ex Ch. Bel-Reve's Eve Of Lifelong. Born 12/14/91, dog. *Judge:* Mrs. Alice Downey.
AKC Record: 46 Bests of Breed; 11 Group placements.

The Belgian Sheepdog is a well balanced, square dog, elegant in appearance with an exceedingly proud carriage of the head and neck. The Belgian Sheepdog should reflect the qualities of intelligence, courage, alertness and devotion to master. To his inherent aptitude as a guardian of flocks should be added protectiveness of the person and property of his master. He should be watchful, attentive, and always in motion when not under command. In his relationship with humans, he should be observant and vigilant with strangers, but not apprehensive. He should not show fear or shyness. He should not show viciousness by unwarranted or unprovoked attack. With those he knows well, he is most affectionate and friendly, zealous of their attention and very possessive. Dogs, 24 to 26 inches; bitches, 22 to 24 inches.

BELGIAN TERVUREN

Ch. Corsairs Wizard

Breeder: Steve Sorenson. *Owners:* Judy Baumeister and Steve Sorenson (Eau Claire, WI). *Handler:* Sherri Samel. By Ch. Corsair's Beaujangles ex Ch. Corsair's Hellon Wheels. Born 05/21/87, dog. *Judge:* Mrs. Alice Downey.
AKC Record: 135 Bests of Breed, including Westminster Kennel Club 1993; 84 Group placements; 3 Bests in Show.

The Belgian Tervuren is a well balanced, square dog, elegant in appearance with an exceedingly proud carriage of the head and neck. The Belgian Tervuren should reflect the qualities of intelligence, courage, alertness and devotion to master. To his inherent aptitude as a guardian of flocks should be added protectiveness of the person and property of his master. He should be watchful, attentive, and always in motion when not under command. In his relationship with humans, he should be observant and vigilant with strangers, but not apprehensive. He should not show fear or shyness. He should not show viciousness by unwarranted or unprovoked attack. With those he knows well, he is most affectionate and friendly, zealous of their attention and very possessive. Dogs, 24 to 26 inches; bitches, 22 to 24 inches.

BOUVIER DES FLANDRES

Ch. Quiche's Nite Ryder

Breeders: Jeffrey Bennett and Nan Eisley-Bennett. *Owners:* Jeffrey Bennett and Nan Eisley-Bennett (Corona, CA). *Handler:* Corky Vroom. By Ch. Zarco Iris VD Cerberushof ex Ch. Laurendell's Gidget de Quiche. Born 02/14/89, dog. *Judge:* Mrs. Marilyn Biggs.
AKC Record: 119 Bests of Breed; 94 Group placements; 4 Bests in Show.

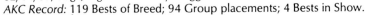

The Bouvier des Flandres is a powerfully built, compact, short-coupled, rough-coated dog of notably rugged appearance. His origin is that of a cattle herder and general farmer's helper, including cart pulling. He is an ideal farm dog. His harsh coat protects him in all weather, enabling him to perform the most arduous tasks. He has been used as an ambulance and messenger dog. Modern times find him as a watch and guard dog as well as a family friend, guardian and protector. His physical and mental characteristics and deportment, coupled with his olfactory abilities, his intelligence and initiative, enable him to also perform as a tracking dog and a guide dog for the blind. Dogs, 24½ to 27½ inches; bitches, 23½ to 26½ inches.

BRIARD

Ch. Bradir Fox Lair Dangerfield

Breeder: Valerie Fox. *Owners:* Valerie Fox and Kenneth Fox (Clinton, MD). *Handler:* Brian W. Meyer. By Virage Vendetta of Picador ex Ch. Dansr Tricot. Born 03/21/88, dog. *Judge:* Mrs. Alice Downey. *AKC Record:* 268 Bests of Breed; 187 Group placements; 5 Bests in Show.

A dog of handsome form. Vigorous and alert, powerful without coarseness, strong in bone and muscle, exhibiting the strength and agility required of the herding dog. He is a dog at heart, with spirit and initiative, wise and fearless with no trace of timidity. Intelligent, easily trained, faithful, gentle, and obedient, the Briard possesses an excellent memory and an ardent desire to please his master. He retains a high degree of his ancestral instinct to guard home and master. Although he is reserved with strangers, he is loving and loyal to those he knows. Some will display a certain independence. Dogs, 23 to 27 inches; bitches, 22 to 25½ inches.

COLLIE (ROUGH)

Ch. Countryview Golden Starr

Breeders: P. Durazzano and D. Cardoza. *Owners:* William Carter and P. Durazzano (Woburn, MA).
Handler: Diane P. Steele. By Ch. Tartanside The Critics Choice ex Starrs Dark Crystal. Born 07/06/89, dog.
Judge: Mrs. Judith A. Goodin.
AKC Record: 77 Bests of Breed; 7 Group placements.

The Collie is a lithe, strong, responsive, active dog, carrying no useless timber, standing naturally straight and firm. The Collie presents an impressive, proud picture of true balance, each part being in harmonious proportion to every other part and to the whole. Expression (which is desirably "sweet") is one of the most important points in considering the relative value of Collies. Dogs, 24 to 26 inches, 60 to 75 pounds; bitches, 22 to 24 inches, 50 to 65 pounds.

COLLIE (SMOOTH)

GROUP
3

Ch. Tedjoi D'Artagnan

Breeder: Joyce Beddow. *Owners:* Duncan C. and Libby Beiler (Milton, PA). *Handler:* Duncan C. Beiler. By Ch. Storm's Grandslam ex Ch. Tedjoi Diamond Tiara. Born 10/15/87, dog. *Judge:* Mrs. Judith A. Goodin. *AKC Record:* 86 Bests of Breed; 18 Group placements; 1 Best in Show.

The Collie is a lithe, strong, responsive, active dog, carrying no useless timber, standing naturally straight and firm. The Collie presents an impressive, proud picture of true balance, each part being in harmonious proportion to every other part and to the whole. Expression (which is desirably "sweet") is one of the most important points in considering the relative value of Collies. Dogs, 24 to 26 inches, 60 to 75 pounds; bitches, 22 to 24 inches, 50 to 65 pounds.

GERMAN SHEPHERD DOG

GROUP 1

Ch. Altana's Mystique

Breeder: M. Charleton. *Owner:* Jane A. Firestone (Roswell/GA). *Handler:* James A. Moses. By Ch. Proven Hills Up N Adam by ex Ch. Covy Altana of Tucker Hill. Born 05/05/87, bitch. *Judge:* Mrs. Joan Schurr Kefeli. *AKC Record:* 335 Bests of Breed, including Westminster Kennel Club 1993; 315 Group placements, including Group 1 Westminster Kennel Club 1993; 192 Bests in Show.

The first impression of a good German Shepherd Dog is that of a strong, agile, well muscled animal, alert and full of life. The breed has a distinct personality marked by direct and fearless, but not hostile, expression, self-confidence and a certain aloofness that does not lend itself to immediate and indiscriminate friendships. The dog must be approachable, quietly standing its ground and showing confidence and willingness to meet overtures without itself making them. It is poised, but when the occasion demands, eager and alert; both fit and willing to serve in its capacity as companion, watchdog, blind leader, herding dog, or guardian, which the circumstances demand. Dogs, 24 to 26 inches; bitches, 22 to 24 inches.

OLD ENGLISH SHEEPDOG

Ch. Lambluv's Winning Maid Easy

Breeder: Jere Marder. *Owner:* Jere Marder (Chicago, IL). *Handler:* Nina Work. By Ch. To-Jo's Nice N'Easy ex Ch. Rholenwood's Taylor Maid. Born 03/10/89, bitch. *Judge:* Mrs. Joan Schurr Kefeli. *AKC Record:* 98 Bests of Breed; 84 Group placements; 7 Bests in Show.

A strong, compact, square, balanced dog. Taking him all around, he is profusely, *but not excessively coated,* thickset, muscular and able bodied. These qualities, combined with his agility, fit him for the demanding tasks required of a shepherd's or drover's dog. An adaptable, intelligent dog of even disposition, with no sign of aggression, shyness or nervousness. Dogs, 22 inches; bitches, 21 inches.

PULI

Ch. Tordor's Gyorgy Dij HT

Breeders: Barbara H. Stelz and Linn Hiett. *Owners:* Beverly and Donald Zeman and Ann Bowley (Pottstown, PA). *Handler:* Ann Bowley. By Ch. Szeder's Lokoto Lacko ex HC Ch. Mt. Hood's Lenke of Tordor CD. Born 12/17/87, dog. *Judge:* Mrs. Joan Schurr Kefeli.
AKC Record: 148 Bests of Breed; 65 Group placements.

The Puli is a compact, square appearing, well balanced dog of medium size. He is vigorous, alert and active. Striking and highly characteristic is the shaggy coat which, combined with his light-footed, distinctive movement, has fitted him for the strenuous work of herding flocks on the plains of Hungary. Agility, combined with soundness of mind and body, is of prime importance for the proper fulfillment of this centuries-old task. By nature an affectionate, intelligent and home-loving companion, the Puli is sensibly suspicious and therefore an excellent watchdog. Dogs, ideally 17 inches; bitches, 16 inches.

SHETLAND SHEEPDOG

Ch. Kates The Marquis O Jopavist

Breeders: Leonard W. Abrahamson and Josephine Abrahamson. *Owners:* Joanne Descoteaux, Joyce Wilkinson and Nancy Runyon (Litchfield, NH). *Handler:* Nancy L. Runyon. By Ch. Minos The Dark Crusader ex Shelturn Jopavist Safari. Born 03/30/90, dog. *Judge:* Mrs. Anne H. Bowes.
AKC Record: 4 Bests of Breed; 1 Group placement.

The Shetland Sheepdog, like the Collie, traces to the Border Collie of Scotland, which, transported to the Shetland Islands and crossed with small, intelligent, longhaired breeds, was reduced to miniature proportions. Subsequently crosses were made from time to time with Collies. This breed now bears the same relationship in size and general appearance to the Rough Collie as the Shetland Pony does to some of the larger breeds of horses. The Shetland Sheepdog is intensely loyal, affectionate, and responsive to his owner. However, he may be reserved toward strangers but not to the point of showing fear or cringing in the ring. Dogs and bitches, 13 to 16 inches.

WELSH CORGI (CARDIGAN)

Am. and Can. Ch. Aragorn's Lord Alden

Breeders: Marieann and Steve Gladstone and Carol Hurlihy. *Owner:* Tom Adamski (New York, NY). *Handler:* Nina Work. By Ch. Aragorn's Silver Wizard ex Ch. Aragorn's Corazon. Born 02/10/90, dog. *Judge:* Mrs. Joan Schurr Kefeli.
AKC Record: 57 Bests of Breed; 6 Group placements.

A handsome, powerful, small dog, capable of both speed and endurance, intelligent, sturdily built but not coarse. In temperament, even-tempered, loyal, affectionate and adaptable. Never shy nor vicious. Dogs, 10½ to 12½ inches, 30 to 38 pounds; bitches, 10½ to 12½ inches, 25 to 34 pounds.

WELSH CORGI (PEMBROKE)

Ch. Nebriowa Face To Face

Breeders: Mrs. Alan R. Robson and Ruth L. Cooper. *Owners:* Mrs. Alan R. Robson and Ruth L. Cooper (Glenview, IL). *Handler:* Michael E. Scott. By Ch. Nebriowa Greenforest Ranger ex Ch. Nebriowa Stitch In Time. Born 09/26/91, dog. *Judge:* Mrs. Anne H. Bowes.
AKC Record: 16 Bests of Breed; 7 Group placements.

Low-set strong, sturdily built and active, giving an impression of substance and stamina in a small space. Outlook bold, but kindly. Expression intelligent and interested. Dogs, 10 to 12 inches, approximately 27 pounds; bitches, 10 to 12 inches, approximately 25 pounds.

WKC BEST IN SHOW AWARDS

1907	Winthrop Rutherfurd—Ch. Warren Remedy, Smooth Fox Terrier
1908	Winthrop Rutherfurd—Ch. Warren Remedy, Smooth Fox Terrier
1909	Winthrop Rutherfurd—Ch. Warren Remedy, Smooth Fox Terrier
1910	Sabine Kennels—Ch. Sabine Rarebit, Smooth Fox Terrier
1911	A. Albright, Jr.—Ch. Tickle Em Jock, Scottish Terrier
1912	William P. Wolcott—Ch. Kenmare Sorceress, Airedale Terrier
1913	Alex H. Stewart—Ch. Strathtay Prince Albert, Bulldog
1914	Mrs. Tylor Morse—Ch. Slumber, Old English Sheepdog
1915	George W. Quintard—Ch. Matford Vic, Wire Fox Terrier
1916	George W. Quintard—Ch. Matford Vic, Wire Fox Terrier
1917	Mrs. Roy A. Rainey—Ch. Conejo Wycollar Boy, Wire Fox Terrier
1918	R.H. Elliot—Ch. Haymarket Faultless, Bull Terrier
1919	G.L. Davis—Ch. Briergate Bright Beauty, Airedale Terrier
1920	Mrs. Roy A. Rainey—Ch. Conejo Wycollar Boy, Wire Fox Terrier
1921	William T. Payne—Ch. Midkiff Seductive, Cocker Spaniel
1922	Frederic C. Hodd—Ch. Boxwood Barkentine, Airedale Terrier
1923	There was no BEST IN SHOW award this year.
1924	Bayard Warren—Ch. Barberryhill Bootlegger, Sealyham Terrier
1925	Robert F. Maloney—Ch. Governor Moscow, Pointer
1926	Halleston Kennels—Ch. Signal Circuit of Halleston, Wire Fox Terrier
1927	Frederic C. Brown—Ch. Pinegrade Perfection, Sealyham Terrier
1928	R.M. Lewis—Ch. Talavera Margaret, Wire Fox Terrier
1929	Mrs. Florence B. Ilch-Laund Loyalty of Bellhaven, Collie
1930	John G. Bates—Ch. Pendley Calling of Blarney, Wire Fox Terrier
1931	John G. Bates—Ch. Pendley Calling of Blarney, Wire Fox Terrier
1932	Giralda Farms—Ch. Nancolleth Markable, Pointer
1933	S.M. Stewart—Ch. Warland Protector of Shelterock, Airedale Terrier
1934	Halleston Kennels—Ch. Flornell Spicy Bit of Halleston, Wire Fox Terrier
1935	Blakeen Kennels—Ch. Nunsoe Duc de la Terrace of Blakeen, Standard Poodle
1936	Claredale Kennels—Ch. St. Margaret Mignificent of Claredale, Sealyham Terrier
1937	Halleston Kennels—Ch. Flornell Spicey, Piece of Halleston, Wire Fox Terrier
1938	Maridor Kennels—Ch. Daro of Maridor, English Setter
1939	Giralda Farms—Ch. Ferry v. Rauhfelsen of Giralda, Doberman Pinscher
1940	H.E. Mellenthin—Ch. My Own Brucie, Cocker Spaniel
1941	H.E. Mellenthin—Ch. My Own Brucie, Cocker Spaniel
1942	Mrs. J.G. Winant—Ch. Wolvey Pattern of Edgerstoune, West Highland White Terrier
1943	Mrs. P.H.B. Frelinghuysen—Ch. Pitter Patter of Piperscroft, Miniature Poodle
1944	Mrs. Edward P. Alker-Flornell-Rare-Bit of Twin Ponds, Welsh Terrier
1945	Mr. & Mrs. T.H. Snethern—Ch. Shieling's Signature, Scottish Terrier
1946	Mr. & Mrs. T.H. Carruthers III—Ch. Heatherington Model Rhythm, Wire Fox Terrier
1947	Mr. & Mrs. Richard C. Kettles, Jr.—Ch. Warlord of Mazelaine, Boxer
1948	Mr. & Mrs. William A. Rockefeller—Ch. Rock Ridge Night Rocket, Bedlington Terrier
1949	Mr. & Mrs. John Phelps Wagner—Ch. Mazelaine Zazarac Brandy, Boxer

1950	Mrs. J.G. Winant—Ch. Walsing Winning Trick of Edgerstoune, Scottish Terrier
1951	Dr. & Mrs. R.C. Harris—Ch. Bang Away of Sirrah Crest, Boxer
1952	Mr. & Mrs. Len Carey—Ch. Rancho Dobe's Storm, Doberman Pinscher
1953	Mr. & Mrs. Len Carey—Ch. Rancho Dobe's Storm, Doberman Pinscher
1954	Mrs. Carl E. Morgan—Ch. Carmor's Rise and Shine, Cocker Spaniel
1955	John A. Saylor, MD—Ch. Kippax Feamought, Bulldog
1956	Bertha Smith—Ch. Wilber White Swan, Toy Poodle
1957	Sunny Shay and Dorothy Chenade—Ch. Shirkhan of Grandeur, Afghan Hound
1958	Puttencove Kennels—Ch. Puttencove Promise, Standard Poodle
1959	Dunwalke Kennels—Ch. Fontclair Festoon, Miniature Poodle
1960	Mr. & Mrs. C.C. Venable—Ch. Chik T'Sun of Caversham, Pekingese
1961	Miss Florence Michelson—Ch. Cappoquin Little Sister, Toy Poodle
1962	Wishing Well Kennels—Ch. Elfinbrook Simon, West Highland White Terrier
1963	Mrs. W.J.S. Borie—Ch. Wakefield's Black Knight, English Springer Spaniel
1964	Pennyworth Kennels—Ch. Courtenay Fleetfoot of Pennyworth, Whippet
1965	Mr. & Mrs. Charles C. Stalter—Ch. Carmichaels Fanfare, Scottish Terrier
1966	Marion G. Bunker—Ch. Zeloy, Mooremaide's Magic, Wire Fox Terrier
1967	E.H. Stuart—Ch. Bardene Bingo, Scottish Terrier
1968	Mr. & Mrs. James A. Farrell, Jr.—Ch. Stingray of Derryabah, Lakeland Terrier
1969	Walter F. Goodman & Mrs. Adele Goodman—Ch. Glamoor Good News, Skye Terrier
1970	Dr. & Mrs. P.J. Pagano & Dr. Theodore Fickes—Ch. Arriba's Prima Donna, Boxer
1971	Milton E. Prickett—Ch. Chinoe's Adamant James, English Springer Spaniel
1972	Milton E. Prickett—Ch. Chinoe's Adamant James, English Springer Spaniel
1973	Edward Jenner & Jo Ann Sering—Ch. Acadia Command Performance, Standard Poodle
1974	Richard P. Smith, MD—Ch. Gretchenhof Columbia River, German Shorthaired Pointer
1975	Mr. & Mrs. R. Vanword—Ch. Sir Lancelot of Barvan, Old English Sheepdog
1976	Mrs. V.K. Dickson—Ch. Jo Ni's Red Baron of Crofton, Lakeland Terrier
1977	Pool Forge Kennels—Ch. Dersade Bobby's Girl, Sealyham Terrier
1978	Barbara A. & Charles W. Switzer—Ch. Cede Higgins, Yorkshire Terrier
1979	Mrs. Anne E. Snelling—Ch. Oak Tree's Irishtocrat, Irish Water Spaniel
1980	Kathleen Kanzler—Ch. Innisfree's Sierra Cinnar, Siberian Husky
1981	Robert A. Hauslohner—Ch. Dhandys Favorite Woodchuck, Pug
1982	Mrs. Anne E. Snelling—Ch. St. Aubrey Dragonora of Elsdon, Pekingese
1983	Chris & Marguerite Terrell—Ch. Kabiks The Challenger, Afghan Hound
1984	Seaward Kennels, Reg.—Ch. Seaward's Blackbeard, Newfoundland
1985	Sonnie & Alan Novick—Ch. Braeburn's Close Encounter, Scottish Terrier
1986	Mrs. Alan R. Robson & Michael Zollo—Ch. Marjetta's National Acclaim, Pointer
1987	Shirlee Braunstein & Jane A. Firestone—Ch. Covy Tucker Hill's Manhattan, German Shepherd Dog
1988	Skip Piazza & Olga Baker—Ch. Great Elms Prince Charming, II, Pomeranian
1989	Richard & Carolyn Vida, Beth Wilhite & Arthur & Susan Korp—Ch. Royal Tudor's Wild As The Wind, Doberman Pinscher
1990	Edward B. Jenner—Ch. Wendessa Crown Prince, Pekingese
1991	Dr. & Mrs. Frederick Hartsock—Ch. Whisperwind On Carousel, Standard Poodle
1992	Marion W. & Samuel B. Lawrence—Ch. Registry's Lonesome Dove, Wire Fox Terrier
1993	Donna S. & Roger H. Herzig, MD, & Julia Gasow—Ch. Salilyn's Condor, English Springer Spaniel
1994	Ruth L. Cooper & Patricia P. Lussier-Forrest—Ch. Chidley Willum The Conqueror, Norwich Terrier

NATIONAL BREED CLUBS

For more information about a particular breed, please contact the following:

SPORTING GROUP

American Brittany Club, Inc. — Secretary, Ms. Joy Watkins, Route 1, Box 114BB, Aledo, TX 76008.

American Pointer Club, Inc. — Secretary, Ms. Lee Ann Stagg, Route 1, Box 10, Branch, LA 70516.

German Shorthaired Pointer Club of America — Secretary, Ms. Geraldine A. Irwin, 1101 West Quincy, Englewood, CO 80110.

German Wirehaired Pointer Club of America, Inc. — Secretary, Ms. Barbara Hein, 3838 Davison Lake Rd., Ortonville, MI 48462.

American Chesapeake Club, Inc. — Secretary, Mr. Janel E. Hopp, 1705 Road 76, Pasco, WA 99301.

Curly-Coated Retriever Club of America — Corres. Secretary, Gina Columbo, 24 Holmes Blvd., Ft. Walton Beach, FL 32548.

Flat-Coated Retriever Society of America, Inc. — Secretary, Ann Mortenson, 6608 Lynwood Blvd., Richfield, MN 55423-2223.

Golden Retriever Club of America — Secretary, Ms. Ginny Kell, 4387 W. Highway 94, Marthasville, MO 63357.

Labrador Retriever Club, Inc. — Corres. Secretary, Mr. Christopher G. Wincek, 9690 Wilson Mills Rd., Chardon, OH 44024.

English Setter Association of America, Inc. — Secretary, Mrs. Dawn S. Ronyak, 114 So. Burlington Oval Dr., Chardon, OH 44024.

Gordon Setter Club of America, Inc. — Secretary, Ms. L. Alison Rosskamp, 945 Font Rd., Glenmoore, PA 19343.

Irish Setter Club of America, Inc. — Corres. Secretary, Mrs. Marion J. Pahy, 16717 Ledge Falls, San Antonio, TX 78232.

American Water Spaniel Club — Secretary, Linda Hattrem, E. 2870 Cedar Rd., Eleva, WI 54738.

Clumber Spaniel Club of America, Inc. — Secretary, Ms. Barbara Stebbins, 9 Cedar St., Selden, NY 11784.

American Spaniel Club, Inc. —Corres. Secretary, Mrs. Margaret M. Ciezkowski, 846 Old Stevens Creek Rd., Martinez, GA 30907-9227.

English Cocker Spaniel Club of America, Inc. — Secretary, Mrs. Kate D. Romanski, P.O. Box 252, Hales Corners, WI 53130.

English Springer Spaniel Field Trial Association, Inc. — Corres. Secretary, Ms. Marie L. Andersen, 29512 47th Ave. So., Auburn, WA 98001.

Field Spaniel Society of America — Corres. Secretary, Ms. Sally Herweyer, 11197 Keystone, Lowell, MI 49331.

Irish Water Spaniel Club of America — Secretary, Ms. Renae Peterson, 24712 SE 380th, Enumclaw, WA 98022.

Sussex Spaniel Club of America — Corres. Secretary, Joan Dunn, N3 W31535 Twin Oaks Dr., Delafield, WI 53018.

Welsh Springer Spaniel Club of America, Inc. — Corres. Secretary, Ms. Karen Lyle, 4425 North 147th St., Brookfield, WI 53005.

Vizsla Club of America, Inc.— Corres. Secretary, Ms. Jan Bouman, 15744 Hampshire Ave. S., Prior Lake, MN 55372.

Weimaraner Club of America — Corres. Secretary, Mrs. Dorothy Derr, P.O. Box 110708, Nashville, TN 37222-0708.

American Wirehaired Pointing Griffon Association — Corres. Secretary, Denny Smith, 90566 Coburg Rd., Eugene, OR 97401.

HOUND GROUP

Afghan Hound Club of America, Inc. — Corres. Secretary, Ms. Norma Cozzoni, 2408A Route 31, Oswego, IL 60543.

Basenji Club of America, Inc. — Secretary, Ms. Susan Patterson-Wilson, P.O. Box 1076, South Bend, IN 46624.

Basset Hound Club of America, Inc. — Secretary, Ms. Andrea Field, 2343 Peters Rd., Ann Arbor, MI 48103.

National Beagle Club — Secretary, Mr. Joseph B. Wiley, Jr., River Rd., Bedminster, NJ 07921.

American Black & Tan Coonhound Club, Inc. — Corres. Secretary, Victoria Blackburn, 700 Grand Ave., Elgin, IL 60120.

American Bloodhound Club — Secretary, Mr. Ed Kilby, 1914 Berry Lane, Daytona Beach, FL 32124.

Borzoi Club of America. Inc.— Corres. Secretary, Mrs. Karen Mays, 29 Crown Dr., Warren, NJ 07059.

Dachshund Club of America, Inc. — Secretary, Mr. Walter M. Jones, 390 Eminence Pike, Shelbyville, KY 40065.

American Foxhound Club — Secretary, Mrs. Jack H. Heck, 1221 Oakwood Ave., Dayton, OH 45419.

Greyhound Club of America — Secretary, Ms. Patricia A. Clark, 227 Hattertown Rd., Newton, CT 06470.

Ibizan Hound Club of the United States — Secretary, Lisa Puskas, 4312 E. Nisbet Rd., Phoenix, AZ 85032.

Irish Wolfhound Club of America — Secretary, Mrs. William S. Pfarrer, 8855 US Route 40, New Carlisle, OH 45344.

Norwegian Elkhound Association of America, Inc. — Corres. Secretary, Mrs. Diane Coleman, 4772 Mentzer Church Rd., Convoy, OH 45832.

Otter Hound Club of America —Corres. Secretary, Dian Quist-Sulek, Route 1, Box 247, Palmyra, NE 68418.

Petit Basset Griffon Vendeen Club of America — Secretary, Ms. Shirley Knipe, 426 Laguna Way, Simi Valley, CA 93065.

Pharaoh Hound Club of America —Corres. Secretary, Rita L. Sacks, Route 209, Box 285, Stone Ridge, NY 12484.

Rhodesian Ridgeback Club of the United States, Inc. — Corres. Secretary, Ms. Betty Epperson, P.O. Box 121817, Ft. Worth, TX 76121-1817.

Saluki Club of America — Secretary, Ms. Marilyn LaBrache Brown, P.O. Box 753, Mercer Island, WA 98040.

Scottish Deerhound Club of America, Inc. — Secretary, Mrs. Joan Shagan, 545 Cummings Lane, Cottontown, TN 37048.

American Whippet Club, Inc. — Secretary, Mrs. Harriett Nash Lee, 14 Oak Circle, Charlottesville, VA 22901.

WORKING GROUP

Akita Club of America — Secretary, Nancy J. Henry, 761 Lonesome Dove Lane, Copper Canyon, TX 75067-8599.

Alaskan Malamute Club of America, Inc. — Corres., Secretary, Ms. Sharon Weston, 187 Grouse Creek Rd., Grants Pass, OR 97526.

Bernese Mountain Dog Club of America, Inc. — Secretary, Ms. Jane Mielke, 156 Hillview Dr., Sullivan, WI 53178.

American Boxer Club, Inc. — Corres. Secretary, Mrs. Barbara E. Wagner, 6310 Edward Dr., Clinton, MD 20735-4135.

American Bullmastiff Association, Inc. — Secretary, Ms. Zoe Murphy, 13850 Forsythe Rd., Sykesville, MD 21784-5811.

Doberman Pinscher Club of America — Corres. Secretary, Ms. Judy Reams, 10316 NE 136th Place, Kirkland, WA 98034.

Giant Schnauzer Club of America, Inc. — Secretary, Ms. Dorothy Wright, 4220 S. Wallace, Chicago, IL 60609.

Great Dane Club of America, Inc. — Corres. Secretary, Mrs. Marie A. Fint, 442 Country View Lane, Garland, TX 75043.

Great Pyrenees Club of America, Inc. — Secretary, Mrs. Charlotte Perry, Route 1, Box 119, Midland, VA 22728.

Komondor Club of America, Inc. — Corres. Secretary, Ms. Sandra Hanson, W359 S10708 Nature Rd., Eagle, WI 53119.

Kuvasz Club of America — Corres. Secretary, Mr. John R. Fulkerson, 16603 SW 5th Place, Newberry, FL 32669.

Mastiff Club of America, Inc. — Corres. Secretary, Ms. Carla Sanchez, 45935 Via Esparanza Temecula, CA 92590.

Newfoundland Club of America, Inc. — Corres. Secretary, Mr. Clyde E. Dunphy, RR 3, Box 155, Carlinville, IL 62626.

Portuguese Water Dog Club of America, Inc. — Corres. Secretary, L. Ann Moore, 16 Auspice Circle, Newark, DE 19711.

American Rottweiler Club — Secretary, Ms. Doreen LePage, 960 South Main St., Pascoag, RI 02859.

St. Bernard Club of America, Inc. — Corres. Secretary, Ms. Carole A. Wilson, 719 East Main St., Belleville, IL 62220.

Samoyed Club of America, Inc. — Corres. Secretary, Ms. Kathie Lensen, W6434 Francis Rd., Cascade, WI 53011.

Siberian Husky Club of America, Inc. — Corres. Secretary, Ms. Carol A. Nash, 54 Newton Rd., Plaistow, NH 03865.

Standard Schnauzer Club of America — Secretary, Ms. Kathy A. Donovan, 4 Deerfield Rd., Brookfield, CT 06804.

TERRIER GROUP

Airedale Terrier Club of America — Secretary, Dr. Suzanne H. Hampton, 47 Tulip Ave., Ringwood, NJ 07456.

Staffordshire Terrier Club of America —

Secretary, H. Richard Pascoe, 785 Valley View Rd., Forney, TX 75126.

Australian Terrier Club of America, Inc. — Corres. Secretary, Ms. Marilyn Harban, 1515 Davon Lane, Nassau Bay, TX 77058,

Bedlington Terrier Club of America — Corres. Secretary, Ms. Carole Anne Diehl, 604 Lafayette Lane, Altoone, PA 16602.

Border Terrier Club of America, Inc. — Secretary, Mrs. Laurale Stern, 832 Lincoln Blvd., Manitowoc, WI 54220.

Bull Terrier Club of America — Corres. Secretary, Mrs. Betty Desmond, Road 2, Box 315, Claysville, PA 15323-9406.

Cairn Terrier Club of America — Corres. Secretary, Mrs. Susan Yertz Millward, 3149 Arkona Rd., Saline, MI 48176.

Dandie Dinmont Terrier Club of America, Inc. — Secretary, Mrs. Mixon M. Darracott, 25 Ridgeview Rd., Staunton, VA 24401.

American Fox Terrier Club — Secretary, Mr. Martin Goldstein, P.O. Box 604, South Plainfield, NJ 07080.

Irish Terrier Club of America — Secretary, Mr. Bruce Petersen, RR 3, Box 449, Bloomington, IL 61704.

United States Kerry Blue Terrier Club, Inc. — Secretary, Ms. Barbara Beuter, 2458 Eastridge Dr., Hamilton, OH 45011.

United States Lakeland Terrier Club — Secretary, Ms. Carol Griffin, P.O. Box 214, Bayport, NY 11705.

American Manchester Terrier Club — Secretary, Ms. Diana Haywood, ROAD2, Box 208A, Hampton Rd., Pittstown, NJ 08867.

Miniature Bull Terrier Club of America — Secretary, Marilyn Drewes, 16 Fremont Rd., Sandown, NH 03873.

American Miniature Schnauzer Club, Inc. — Secretary, Mrs. Susan R. Atherton, RR 2, Box 3570, Bartlesville, OK 74003.

Norwich and Norfolk Terrier Club — Corres. Secretary, Mrs. Maurice J. Matteson, 407 Grenoble Dr., Sellersville, PA 18960.

Scottish Terrier Club of America — Corres. Secretary, Mrs. Diane Zollinger, P.O. Box 1893, Woodinville, WA 98072.

American Sealyham Terrier Club — Secretary, Mrs. Barbara Carmany, Box 76, Sharon Center, OH 44274.

Skye Terrier Club of America — Secretary, Mrs. Karen Sanders, 11567 Sutters Mill Circle, Gold River, CA 95670.

Soft Coated Wheaten Terrier Club of America — Corres. Secretary, Mrs. Mary Anne Dallas, 4607 Willow Lane, Nazareth, PA 18064.

Staffordshire Bull Terrier Club, Inc. — Corres. Secretary, Linda Barker, P.O. Box 70213, Knoxville, TN 37918-7000.

Welsh Terrier Club of America, Inc. — Corres. Secretary, Ms. Helen Chamides, 698 Ridge Rd., Highland Park, IL 60035.

West Highland White Terrier Club of America — Corres. Secretary, Ms. Anne Sanders, 33101 44th Ave. NW, Stanwood, WA 98292.

TOY GROUP

Affenpinscher Club of America — Corres. Secretary, Ms. Terry B. Graham, 2006 Scenic Rd., Tallahassee, FL 32303.

American Brussels Griffon Association — Secretary., Mr. Terry J. Smith, Box 56,221 E.

Scott, Grand Ledge, MI 48837.

Chihuahua Club of America, Inc. — Corres. Secretary, Ms. Lynnie Bunten, 5019 Village Trail, San Antonio, TX 78218.

American Chinese Crested Club, Inc. — Corres. Secretary, Ms. Lynda McMillian, 3101 East Blount St., Pensacola, FL 32503.

English Toy Spaniel Club of America — Corres. Secretary, Ms. Susan Jackson, 18451 Sheffield Lane, Bristol, IN 46507-9455.

Italian Greyhound Club of America, Inc. — Corres. Secretary, Ms. Jamie Daily, 13403 Lacewood, San Antonio, TX 78233.

Japanese Chin Club of America — Secretary, Ms. Faith G. Milton, 2113 Tract Rd., Fairfield, PA 17320-9235.

American Maltese Association, Inc. — Corres. Secretary, Ms. Pamela G. Rightmyer, 6145 Coley Ave., Las Vegas, NV 89102.

American Manchester Terrier Club — Secretary, Ms. Diana Haywood, ROAD2, Box 208A, Hampton Rd., Pittstown, NJ 08867.

Miniature Pinscher Club of America, Inc. — Secretary, Mrs. Kay Phillips, Route 1, Box 173, Temple, TX 76501.

Papillon Club of America, Inc. — Corres. Secretary, Mrs. Janice Dougherty, 551 Birch Hill Rd., Shoemakersville, PA 19555.

Pekingese Club of America, Inc. — Secretary, Mrs. Leonie Marie Schultz, Route 1, Box 321, Bergton, VA 22811.

American Pomeranian Club, Inc. — Corres. Secretary, Ms. Frances J. Stoll, RR 3, Box 429, Washington, IN 47501.

Poodle Club of America, Inc. — Corres. Secretary, Mrs. Sally Kinne, 2514 Custer Parkway, Richardson, TX 75080.

Pug Dog Club of America, Inc. — Secretary, Mr. James P. Cavallaro, 1820 Shadowlawn St., Jacksonville, FL 32205.

American Shih Tzu Club,. Inc. — Corres. Secretary, Ms. Jo Ann Regelman, 837 Auburn Ave, Ridgewood, NJ 07450.

Silky Terrier Club of America, Inc. — Secretary, Ms. Louise Rosewell, 2783 S. Saulsbury St., Denver, CO 80227.

Yorkshire Terrier Club of America, Inc. — Secretary, Mrs. Betty R. Dullinger, P.O. Box 100, Porter, ME 04068.

NON-SPORTING GROUP

Bichon Frise Club of America, Inc. — Corres. Secretary, Mrs. Bernice D. Richardson, Route 2, Gulch Lane, Twin Falls, ID 83301.

Boston Terrier Club of America, Inc. — Corres. Secretary, Ms. Marian Sheehan, 8537 East San Burno Dr., Scottsdale, AZ 85258.

Bulldog Club of America — Secretary, Ms. Linda Sims, 8810 M St., Omaha, NE 68127.

Chinese Shar-Pei Club of America, Inc. — Secretary, Ms. Jocelyn Barker, 6101 Alpine Woods Dr., Anchorage, AK 99516.

Chow Chow Club, Inc. — Corres. Secretary, Ms. Irene Cartabio, 3580 Plover Place, Seaford, NY 11783.

Dalmatian Club of America, Inc. — Corres. Secretary, Mrs. Anne T. Fleming, 4390 Chickasaw Rd., Memphis, TN 38117.

Finnish Spitz Club of America — Secretary, Connie Britt, 7870 Lakewood Dr., Austin, TX 78750.

French Bulldog Club of America — Corres. Secretary, David F. Kruger, 6336 Berkley Dr., New Orleans, LA 70131-4106.

Keeshond Club of America, Inc. — Corres. Secretary, Ms. Shannon Kelly, 8535 N. 10th Ave., Phoenix, AZ 85021-4414.

American Lhasa Apso Club, Inc. — Secretary, Ms. Amy J. Andrews, 18105 Kirkshire, Birmingham, MI 48025.

Poodle Club of America. Inc. — Corres. Secretary, Mrs. Sally Kinne, 2514 Custer Parkway, Richardson, TX 75080.

Schipperke Club of America, Inc. — Secretary, Ms. Diana Dick, 5205 Chaparral, Laramie, WY 82070.

National Shiba Club of America — Secretary, Frances M. Thorton, 101 Peaceful Dr., Converse, TX 78109.

Tibetan Spaniel Club of America — Corres. Secretary, Ms. Shirley Howard, 29W028 River Glen Rd., West Chicago, IL 60185.

Tibetan Terrier Club of America, Inc. — Secretary, Ms. Brenda Brown, 127 Springlea Dr., Winfield, WV 25213.

HERDING GROUP

Australian Cattle Dog Club of America — Secretary, Billie Johnson, 24605 Lewiston Blvd., Hampton, MN 55031

United States Australian Shepherd Association — Secretary, Sherry Ball, P.O. Box 4317, Irving, TX 75015.

Bearded Collie Club of America, Inc. — Corres. Secretary, Ms. Diana Siebert 1116 Carpenter's Trace, Villa Hills, KY 41017.

American Belgian Malinois Club — Corres. Secretary, Ms. Barbara Peach, 1717 Deer Creek Rd., Central Valley, CA 96019.

Belgian Sheepdog Club of America, Inc. — Corres. Secretary, Mrs. Geraldine B. Kimball, 211 West Elm Street, Pembroke, MA 02359.

American Belgian Tervuren Club, Inc. — Corres. Secretary, Ms. Nancy Carman, 4970 Chinook Trail, Casper, WY 82604.

American Bouvier des Flandres Club, Inc. — Secretary, Ms. Dianne Ring, Route 1, Box 201, Delaplane, VA 22025.

Briard Club of America, Inc. — Secretary, Ms. Janet G. Wall, 547 Sussex Court Elk Grove Village, IL 60007.

Collie Club of America, Inc. — Secretary, Mrs. Carmen Leonard, 1119 South Fleming Rd., Woodstock, IL 60098.

German Shepherd Dog Club of America, Inc. — Corres. Secretary, Miss Blanche Beisswenger, 17 West Ivy Lane, Englewood, NJ 07631.

Old English Sheepdog Club of America, Inc. — Corres. Secretary, Ms. Kathryn L. Bunnell, 14219 E. 79th St. So., Derby, KS 67037.

Puli Club of America, Inc. — Secretary, Ms. Dodie Atkins, 6036 Peachmont Terrace, Norcross, GA 30092.

American Shetland Sheepdog Association — Corres. Secretary, Ms. Susan Beachum, 2125 E. 16th Ave., Post Falls, ID 83854.

Cardigan Welsh Corgi Club of America, Inc. — Corres. Secretary, Dr. Kathleen Harper, 544 Bridletrace Dr., Leeds, AL 35094.

Pembroke Welsh Corgi Club of America, Inc. — Corres. Secretary, Mr. John Vahaly, 1608 Clearview Dr., Louisville, KY 40222.

INDEX